PRAISE FOR
THE BETTER OF THE BAD

"J.J. Hensley has pulled off an incredible feat: *The Better of the Bad* is a real rush with a gripping mystery at its heart. The Trevor Galloway series gets bigger, badder, and more energetic with every book."

—Nick Kolakowski, author of
Boise Longpig Hunting Club
and *Maxine Unleashes Doomsday*

THE BETTER OF THE BAD

BOOKS BY J.J. HENSLEY

Trevor Galloway Thrillers
Bolt Action Remedy
Record Scratch
Forgiveness Dies
The Better of the Bad

Resolve
Measure Twice
Chalk's Outline

J.J. HENSLEY

THE BETTER OF THE BAD
A TREVOR GALLOWAY THRILLER

Copyright © 2020 by J.J. Hensley

All rights reserved. No part of the book may be reproduced in any form or by any electronic or mechanical means, including information storage and retrieval systems, without permission in writing from the publisher, except by a reviewer who may quote brief passages in a review.

Down & Out Books
3959 Van Dyke Road, Suite 265
Lutz, FL 33558
DownAndOutBooks.com

The characters and events in this book are fictitious. Any similarity to real persons, living or dead, is coincidental and not intended by the author.

Cover design by Zach McCain

ISBN: 1-64396-149-7
ISBN-13: 978-1-64396-149-1

For Kasia and Cassie
The best parts of me

As if you could kill time without injuring eternity.
—Henry David Thoreau

Chatham County, Georgia

In her bones, she knew it was too early for her to be flying solo. Two more weeks at the side of a mentor was what she had been told, but that promise had vanished along with so many of the faces with which she had become familiar since taking the job. Those first few days had been stressful enough; everything seemed to be moving at the speed of light. She marveled at how the calls flooded in and grizzled veterans made quick, dispassionate assessments before keying up their microphones to broadcast information in a language that at times seemed foreign. The most experienced among them could take a call made by some dude screaming his head off like he was being chased by a maniac with an axe, get the caller to give the basic information needed for a response, send a unit, and then turn back to the neighboring dispatcher to resume a meaningless conversation about the latest episode of *The Bachelor*. But that was before.

Now, there was no idle chitchat. On the rare instances the Savannah area let the phone lines rest, there was nothing but silence in the dispatch center that somehow still seemed cramped despite some of the stations being empty. Silence was what Denise Warren wanted right now because she didn't know if she could handle anything more difficult than the two calls she'd taken since coming on shift: a small car fire on Bull Street and a report of a homeless man harassing tourists down by the riverfront. On most days, because of the poor layout of the Savannah-Chatham Communications Center, not all the dispatchers were in the same room. However, with so many of the communications officers calling in sick or flat-out quitting, Denise could see all the other dispatchers' anxious expressions. Throughout her abbreviated training, a phrase had been drilled into her: *There are no routine calls.* While she appreciated the sentiment, Denise knew it was mostly bullshit. Routine was the dream. To be competent enough to handle the barrage of phone and radio chatter while keeping your cool was supposed to be the goal. Not tonight. Tonight, the goal was to make it through without getting *the* call.

She glanced up at the fluorescent clock on the wall at the far side of the room. The red digits burned 9:10 PM. As if the rest of the city—hell, the rest of the county—knew, the phones stopped ringing. Nobody made a sound. Not a chair squeak. Not a tap on a keyboard.

Denise examined the faces around her. Elizabeth—a husband and two kids. She'd heard Jake was newlywed. She didn't know Alfonzo well, but the heavy-set man had a wedding band and seemed the family type. Alicia was definitely single. She'd become friendly with Alicia after the two had gone out for drinks one night. After downing a couple of gin and tonics, Alicia had become flirty and tested the waters with Denise. While flattered, Denise politely let her know the winds weren't going to blow that direction, but the two had remained friends. Skyler and the guy everyone just called "T" were total mysteries to her since they were recent emergency additions called in from some adjacent jurisdiction. Patrice, who was a total bitch to all the other women, complained incessantly about her husband, who was retired from the Army and apparently bored out of his mind at home. If Denise remembered correctly, she had two grown kids who were both living somewhere in the area.

The numbers on the clock changed to 9:11 PM. Denise became aware of a low hum from the fans somewhere within the communications consoles. She'd never noticed it before and wondered if anyone ever had since the center was normally a beehive twenty-four hours a day. She watched her screen and then took a few surreptitious peeks at the others who were all doing the same.

Damn. She forgot to count. How many seconds had passed? Twenty? Thirty? No, it had to be more than that because she could see the tension leaving Alfonzo's face. He was starting to nod, and Denise could tell it was part of an inner monologue. He was probably saying something like, *Okay. Okay. It's okay tonight.* Now Elizabeth was also nodding and silently mouthing something, probably a prayer.

Denise stole a look at the clock one more time, knowing it had to have changed by now. It hadn't, but any second now. Any—

Ringggggggggggg

Everyone in the room jolted.

Ringggggggggggg

The readout was on everyone's screen.

9-1-1 Unknown Location/Blocked Number

All eyes went to Elizabeth. As the senior dispatcher, she would be the one to take the call. There was still a realistic chance it was a *routine* 9-1-1 call. They'd had plenty of those from cell phones on or around the designated time on nights when they hadn't gotten *the* call. Elizabeth swallowed hard, adjusted her chair, and wheeled herself a little too close to her console.

"Put it on speaker, please."

Everyone jumped again when the command came from the back of the room.

The wiry man with skin as dark as night repeated his request, which to Denise didn't sound like a request at all. Denise didn't know who the man was, but there was no doubt in her mind that the call was going to be broadcasted throughout the room. She'd seen him hovering on the outskirts of the circles of yellow illumination created by the oversized bulbs in the facility's recessed lighting fixtures on two other occasions, but this was the first time she'd heard him speak.

Elizabeth answered the call and pressed an icon on her screen, allowing the call to be heard by all of them.

"Chatham 9-1-1. What's your emergency?" asked the senior dispatcher.

Dead air.

"Chatham 9-1-1."

Elizabeth looked at the others in the room and finally at the man in the doorway whose face was unreadable.

"Caller, are you there?" she said.

When no response came, she exhaled, not realizing she had been keeping the air in her lungs, and turned toward the console to deactivate the call.

A distorted voice boomed through the speakers.

"Thirteen-Fifty-One Exley Street. Rush, rush, but I bet you won't be on time."

All the eyes in the room began searching—seeking out the individual for whom that address might have meaning.

It meant nothing to Denise, who was already trying to gauge if Elizabeth, who was already visibly shaken, was the one. She was rattled but didn't seem to react to what the caller had said. She turned toward Jake, but he was looking at T and Skyler who appeared to be checking in on each other. Alfonzo. Alfonzo was leaning over in his chair and had his face in his hands. Denise wondered if she should approach him and say something to him. But then, Patrice walked over to him, put a hand on his back, and whispered something in his ear. He raised his head and quietly said the words *not me*.

Denise rotated her chair slowly to the station behind her. Alicia was staring wide-eyed into nothingness, tears streaming down her face. Now everyone focused on the young woman who was becoming aware of the attention.

The man standing in the back of the room said, "What are you waiting for? Dispatch officers to that address now. Advise them to use extreme caution."

Elizabeth wiped a tear from her eye and made the call.

The wiry man walked past Denise to where Alicia was sitting

and knelt down, bringing his six-foot-three frame closer to her level. He spoke softly, but Denise could still hear him.

"Who lives there?" he asked with a calm and evenness Denise had never witnessed from anyone.

"My...my grandmother," Alicia wept.

The man nodded and started to stand.

"And my two cousins."

The man lowered himself again and struggled to keep his expression neutral as he said, "How old are your cousins? Damon and Jeremy."

Through a wave of tears, Alicia said, "Damon's seventeen. Jeremy turned nineteen last week."

The man who Denise had noted was in a suit, not a uniform, stood and rubbed a hand over his clean-shaven head. There was a flash of anger in his eyes, but then it was gone, and Denise saw it had been replaced with something else. She wasn't sure what had pushed the anger away, but the only words that came to Denise's mind were *reason* and *calculation*.

The man strode to Elizabeth's station, put an arm on her shoulder, and said, "Send multiple ambulances there now. Have them hold their positions nearby until the scene is cleared by PD."

Denise watched Elizabeth adjust her headset and take a deep breath. How many times had Elizabeth given these commands over the air during her fifteen-year career, Denise wondered. Five thousand? Ten thousand? Now the woman's hands were trembling, and her voice was cracking as she sent the EMTs to go treat victims that were undoubtedly past the point of help. The comfort of *routine* was long gone, and it didn't seem like it was ever coming back. Denise grabbed her purse, stood, and walked toward the door. She needed a paycheck, but she didn't want any part of this.

Chapter 1

Trevor Galloway
Pittsburgh, Pennsylvania

"You need to breathe," I said, not for the first time.

"I am breathing."

"No. You're on the verge of hyperventilating. Remember our training. When we panic, we make mistakes. You've prepared for this. You've rehearsed this. You know the sequence of events and the timing. It's like any other operation we've worked. Simple clockwork."

"Easy for you to say," Chase Vinson snapped. "I'm the first through this door. I always thought it would be you."

A bead of sweat formed on my friend's forehead. The usually unflappable detective tugged at a too-tight collar as his massive neck threatened to pop the button and unravel the bowtie. I sneaked a glance into the seats and saw Bethany was enjoying every moment of seeing Chase squirm. I should have felt sorry for the man who had taken extraordinary chances and assisted me on countless occasions, but the part of me that is a student of human behavior found his ongoing internal apocalypse fascinating—and, yes, entertaining.

I said, "Don't worry. I'm sure she's as nervous as you. In fact, if she found an open window, she may be out of the city by now."

The muscles around Chase's jaws contracted as he tried not to react, knowing many pairs of eyes were on him.

He looked down toward his feet and mumbled, "I'm getting married to a woman I've known for only six months. This tuxedo feels like it's two sizes too small. And my best man—who is hated by half the people here—stopped taking his medication, so he may or may not experience hallucinations during the ceremony. To top it off, now he suddenly thinks he's funny."

"I'm not funny," I said. "And I *am* honored you asked me to be here with you."

"Shut up," he said. "Just make sure you have the ring ready."

"I'm sure one of us over here has it," I said.

This time, Chase couldn't help but turn to me. There were no groomsmen, so it was only the two of us on our side, the priest in the middle, and a bridesmaid opposite us. My giant friend looked down at me.

"Hallucinations jokes. Now. Really? Maybe Savannah has been *too* good for you."

Life in Savannah had been good to us over the past year. Bethany had become a private investigator, and I joined her by working behind the scenes. Unfortunately, business had been pretty terrible thus far. Other than a few low-level divorce cases and one missing person who showed up before we could collect a fee, we hadn't been able to make Coastal Casework Investigations, or CCI, profitable. It wasn't that we had a bad reputation. In fact, we didn't want to be a high-profile firm. The problem was CCI had *no* reputation in a city that grasped onto legacies the way struggling swimmers latch onto life preservers. On the bright side, we'd been expecting trouble from my past to catch up with us, and it hadn't come. Nothing. Although the absence of danger should have put us at ease, the silence from what Chase liked to call the Eastern European Drug Cartel, or EEDC, was deafening.

The music started and all attention turned toward the back of the church. Bethany and I had just met Lauren Hahm in the days leading up to the wedding, and we liked her immediately. A pediatrician with a practice outside the city, she'd met Chase online and the two had bonded over a mutual love of exercise and an obsession with Alfred Hitchcock movies. While one might think an imposing burglary detective and a soft-spoken suburban doctor would be an odd pairing, the two seemed to be as in love as any couple I'd ever known. Of course, as a former cop and recovering addict in my mid-forties, living with a woman significantly younger, who was I to judge?

As the bride made her way down the aisle in her white dress, I looked on as Chase seemed to finally lose himself in the moment. He watched her approach, and I could sense calm coming over him when he realized he was doing the right thing—which was the case with him nearly all the time. I rarely smile but began to feel the urge right up to the point when I glanced over at Bethany. She was absolutely stunning in her dress, her short, reddish hair standing out among the onlookers consisting mostly of the couple's friends and family. Bethany looked at me, at the bride, then the groom, and back to me. The urge to curl my lips disappeared as she mouthed one word to me—the man who, considering he'd been waiting for a drug gang to assassinate him, hadn't even *thought* about proposing marriage.

It didn't take expert lip-reading skills to interpret the word, and one didn't need years of investigative experience to derive the meaning.

Soon.

Okay, I thought. Apparently, we would be engaged soon. Given Bethany's disregard for tradition, I didn't know if that meant I would be doing the proposing or if she would simply let me know when we were betrothed. Regardless, wedding bells were in our future. While the prospect of getting married didn't bother me one bit, there were other considerations. One issue was the fact we were operating a fledgling business and, while we were being careful with money, the funds left over from our last case wouldn't last forever.

"We are gathered here..." the priest began.

As an investigator, Bethany was a natural. We had a nice, and necessary, arrangement in which Bethany would be the face of CCI and I would work behind the scenes. However, given our dwindling bank account balance and my limited contributions to the enterprise, I was going to have to talk to her about my finding another job. She wasn't going to be happy with the idea, but having me twiddle my thumbs between the few cases we had wasn't going to pay the bills.

"Do you have the ring?" I heard a voice say.

Chase eyed me with apprehension, but I produced the ring.

Then there was the question as to what kind of normal job I could get? I couldn't go back into law enforcement. Forty-something, former narcotics detectives with psychological problems don't get jobs in law enforcement. And all that any government or private sector employer had to do was a quick Google search of my name to discover I'd been locked away in a psychiatric facility for going on what some publications had callously called a "killing spree." I didn't have a LinkedIn profile, but I was relatively sure *Killing Spree* wasn't a popular search term with corporate recruiters.

Being a private investigator, albeit unlicensed, had led me down a dangerous path, and while I felt I'd done some good, I had caused a great deal of pain. Hence, it was important I stay behind the scenes at CCI as to not scare off potential clients. Also, Bethany could keep me from being overly invested in any big cases—should we actually *get* any big cases.

"...man and wife."

Soon, she'd mouthed. *Soon.*

Chapter 2

Trevor Galloway

Although the wedding at the church on Stanwix Street had promised to be organized and tame, the reception around the corner at the hotel on Liberty Avenue made no such vows. In most cases, doctors, nurses, and cops can be entrusted with the lives of total strangers, but the survival of an open bar under those circumstances is asking way too much. As the best man, I was expected to make a toast, although Chase had graciously given me the opportunity to decline that obligation. Feeling I owed Chase more than I could ever repay, I opted to say a few short words in front of a crowd filled with cops who were largely hostile toward me. Remembering I'm not funny, I skipped any attempt at humor, said all the right things about the bride and groom, raised my glass, and took my seat. No harm done. With any luck, Bethany and I could skip out after a few more minutes and head up to our room. Chase would completely understand if I evaporated into the night.

"You did fine," Bethany said while I leaned in close and kissed her on the cheek as the happy couple started their first dance as husband and wife.

I put my arm around Bethany, and we watched as Chase and Lauren stared into each other's eyes and swayed to a song I didn't recognize. Immediately thereafter, a tearful Lauren danced with her father before Chase danced with his mother. Chase's mother was dwarfed by her son, whose tattoo collection was starting to poke out from the wrists of his dress shirt.

"You never talk about your parents," she said.

"They've been gone a long time."

"But you think about them."

"Sure. From time to time."

"Was your father like you?" she asked. "I bet he was. He probably spent his days looking stoic and staring holes through people."

I turned from the dance floor where everyone was joining in and moving to another song I didn't recognize.

"He was a floor supervisor for a furniture manufacturing company in North Carolina. He wasn't a cop, but I'm sure he could convey commands with little more than a stare."

"So, what was he like?"

"I've told you," I said.

"No. You've coasted by with clichés and I've let you get by with it thus far. But now I want to know."

I faced her. Now it was my tux that felt two sizes too small. Talking about my past, even the decent parts, always made me feel uncomfortable.

"He was a good man and a good father. If I have any criticism of him, it's that although I saw him every day, I didn't know him well. He died right before I went off to college, and some part of me feels like we were strangers."

Bethany took a sip from a wine glass she'd been holding. I'd opted not to have anything more than the courtesy sip of champagne to keep my wits about me in this environment.

"What about your mother?" she asked.

"She was great," I said.

Bethany shook her head and said, "What about your mother?"

I really wasn't going to get by with any cookie-cutter responses.

"There's not much to tell. She liked to try her hand at lots of different things. She'd work one job, then another. I guess she was a restless soul. She used to say her callings always called her elsewhere."

Bethany asked, "And she died your freshman year?"

"My second freshman year."

She smiled. My first freshman year had been at the Virginia Military Institute. However, my temperament wasn't a great fit for the military part of the institution's name, so I ended up at the University of Akron after a slight incident involving assaulting an upperclassman got me kicked out of VMI.

"Hey, I've fulfilled my duties. Is it okay if we get out of here and head up to our room?" I asked hopefully.

"Don't you want to dance?" Bethany asked, taunting me.

"Come on. Let's go," I said, standing up.

"Oh, please," she teased. "I want to see the Tin Man get jiggy wit it."

Bethany stood and nearly spilled her wine as she mimicked something between a robot and the Tin Man from the Wizard of Oz.

"How many glasses of wine have you had?" I asked.

"This is *not* my first," she answered, beaming.

She polished off the rest of her wine and set the glass on an abandoned table.

"You know I can't dance, and you know I won't."

She put on her pouty lips, still toying with me. "Fine. Let's leave."

We made our way around the outside of the banquet room and into the hallway. Bethany stopped me and clasped my arm long enough to slide out of her heels. She carried them as we walked down the corridor lined with a patterned carpet in need of replacing.

"What was your mother like at home?"

I shrugged. "Like I said, she was great."

"Was she happy?"

"It seemed so. On most days, she was upbeat."

I remembered back to my childhood, and what I'd said was true. But for some reason, my answer was gnawing at me. I spoke as I thought it out.

"I mean, she had bad days. It was her restless personality. She'd go off on long drives by herself or go down in our basement and listen to music on our 8-track player. Sometimes I'd come home from school, yell for her, and think she wasn't home. Eventually, I'd find her down there next to the stereo, listening to those old tapes with her headphones on. She used those things even when nobody else was home. She could lose herself in the music. More than once, I tapped her on the shoulder and nearly scared her to death."

I thought Bethany might smile at that image, but her expression had turned serious.

"She always laughed about it when she realized it was me," I said.

"Oh, I'm sure she did," Bethany said.

We turned down a corner leading to where I thought I remembered the elevators being. Nobody else was around, which wasn't the most encouraging sign. I'd hoped to follow at least a few people who might be bailing out of the reception early. Suddenly, I became aware Bethany was being oddly quiet.

"Are you feeling okay?" I asked.

She took a few more strides and started to speak. Before she could get the words out, I felt a shove on the back of my left shoulder.

The shove was accompanied by slurred words. "Hey, asshole!"

I regained my balance, and we both turned toward the two men, each of whom were wearing suits in varying states of post-wedding disarray.

Nice job, Galloway. I thought. *A drug gang wants you dead, and you let two drunken wedding guests sneak up on you.*

"That was a real nice toast you gave," said the guy in the red tie that was loosened at the neck. Erik Drayman. I knew him from my days working drugs in Pittsburgh. We'd gotten along well enough back in those days, but a lot had happened since then and time didn't heal all wounds. Some wounds become scars—permanent reminders of trauma inflicted—what exists is taken and something coarse is left behind.

"So, this is him?" Green Tie asked rhetorically.

Green Tie was at least fifteen years younger than me and had the build of something that would give rodeo clown nightmares. There was a resemblance between him and Drayman. If I had to guess, I'd say the kid was related to Erik and also on the job. Compliments of Erik and others, the kid had probably been bombarded with tales about my fall from grace and subsequent push out the door by the department's brass.

Green Tie stepped close to me, and I could smell bourbon on his breath. The top button of his white shirt was undone, and his Adam's apple was at my eye level. He was probably a SWAT guy. He seemed like a SWAT guy.

"We have to be on our way," I said.

I began to turn away, but Erik stepped in close beside the gorilla and put a finger in my chest. His breath carried the scent of the beer, and the mixture of alcohol odors was starting to annoy me.

Erik said, "You shouldn't have come here, Galloway. You should still be locked up. In fact, you should be dead in the gutter somewhere."

I didn't say anything, hoping my former colleague would get his satisfaction from venting and showing off in front of his younger relative.

He turned his attention to Bethany and said, "Do you know everything he's done, sweetie? Or maybe you don't care because you're getting paid by the hour."

My shoulders sank; I let out a long breath and closed my eyes, knowing what was coming. The mistake both the men made was turning their attention to me after the insult had been flung in

Bethany's direction. During my incarceration, and throughout the first months of my release, I was a heavily medicated, lethargic, physical wasteland. Since around the time I met Bethany, I'd spent a great deal of time getting back into shape and bulking up. Now I was heavier than I'd ever been, but in a good, sturdy way. While the two lugs in front of me might have considered me a potential threat, what they didn't realize was I had been further developing my already formidable fighting skills with a certain redhead who was extremely accomplished in a system of self-defense called Krav Maga.

I heard the crack as I opened my eyes and saw blood pouring out of Erik's nose. He staggered back three steps and nearly lost his footing. Bethany stood there as if nothing had happened, her shoes dangling from her innocent left hand, but I knew her right had lashed out like a cobra, delivering a palm strike to Erik's face. Erik staggered back several yards, somehow maintaining his balance.

The gorilla turned to her and then to me, unsure what to do since he wasn't about to hit a woman.

"Jesus Christ," Erik yelled while hunched over, his hands covering his face.

We all watched as drops of crimson fell through his fingers.

"So, are you his son?" I asked the bigger man whose mouth was agape.

"Sister's kid," he stammered, keeping his eyes on his uncle.

"On the job?"

He nodded. "Gang Task Force."

"Ever on the SWAT team? I pegged you for a SWAT guy."

He gave a nod while watching his uncle dig around in a jacket pocket for something—anything—to help curtail the bleeding.

Through his hands, Erik barked, "Goddamnit, Chris. Get me some napkins or something! I think she broke my damn nose."

Chris lumbered away from us to put an arm on his uncle. He leaned down and mumbled something in Erik's ear before guiding him around a corner, presumably in search of a restroom.

"That went well," I said, turning to Bethany.

"Yeah," she replied almost disinterestedly.

We resumed walking down the hall.

She'd just punched a police officer in the face, and it seemed she couldn't have cared less.

My cell phone rang in my pocket.

"Hey, what's going on with you?" I asked.

"Nothing," she said.

What a relief, I thought. To me, it seemed like something was wrong with the woman I loved, but I asked her if something was going on and she said it was *nothing*. So, obviously *nothing* was going on and all was right with the world. There was absolutely *zero* chance that something could be wrong and that she wasn't telling me this very second.

Of course, I'm not a total idiot, so I knew something was wrong. And I *am* kind of an idiot, so I decided to push the issue. My phone rang again.

"Look, why don't we—"

"Answer your phone."

The expression on her face let me know she was giving me an out, and that I better take it, so I answered the call that was coming from a Savannah number. Our office line rolled over to both our cell phones, and this call appeared to have come through our CCI line. It was after hours, but we had few clients and seldom received calls. I went ahead and answered.

"CCI," I said into the phone as we arrived at the elevators.

"Hello. I...I was expecting to leave a voice mail. Is this the answering service?"

"No, you've reached an associate at CCI. How may we help you?"

"I would like to make an appointment to speak with you regarding a situation."

A *situation*. Fantastic. Another low-dollar domestic case that will begin with nobody wanting to write a check and end with everybody being pissed off.

"We may be able to squeeze you in on Monday?" I lied.

I didn't have to consult our calendar to know Monday was wide open. Tuesday's schedule wasn't exactly a typhoon of activity either.

"I need to speak with you tomorrow," said the man.

It was Saturday. This guy wasn't thinking straight. He'd probably just figured out his wife was stepping out on him and he wanted proof this instant so he could have her dead to rights in court.

Bethany pressed the button to call for the elevator. I glanced down the hallway to make sure Erik and his nephew Chris weren't returning for another go-round. When I looked back at Bethany, she was looking up at the indicator lights above the elevator door and watching them count down to our level. Normally, she was an open book. Suddenly, she was a blurry maze.

"I'm afraid our chief investigator is indisposed at the moment," I responded. "We can set something up as early as Monday mor—"

"People are dying. This can't wait. If you can't meet with me, I'll find someone else."

The elevator doors opened, and Bethany stepped in. I stood halfway in and held the doors open, wanting to make sure I didn't drop the call by getting in the elevator. I did a quick calculation of our flight schedules and estimated arrival time for the next day.

I said, "Ms. Nolan can meet you at our office at six PM. Will that work for you?"

"I'll be there."

"The address is—"

"I'll be there."

The call disconnected.

Focus returned to Bethany's eyes. I moved into the elevator, let the doors shut, and pressed the button for our floor.

"A case?" she asked.

"A case."
"Domestic?"
I shook my head. "I don't think so."

Chapter 3

Trevor Galloway

Bells chimed as the front door swung open, and I could hear heavy footsteps cross the timeworn wooden planks in the foyer. Even though I was seated in the back office with the door closed, I'd have no difficulty hearing the conversation that was about to ensue in Bethany's office. We shared a wall that inexplicably included a large rectangular vent near the floor. The vent, covered by a decorative iron grate, didn't actually *vent* anywhere, although it looked like an air intake. It was little more than a cutout in our common wall.

The dilapidated house we rented and used as an office was in a *transitional* area of Savannah, which meant it wasn't exactly in the hood, but bright orange trollies filled with wide-eyed tourists weren't going to linger outside our door either. The location suited our needs, as we didn't expect to benefit much from walk-in business, so it didn't really matter if we were in a more respectable location. More importantly, the rent was cheap because the landlord figured we weren't selling crack, meth, or heroin.

Lighter footsteps approached from a different direction, and I heard Bethany introduce herself.

"My name is Sebastian Waterford," I heard a man say, and I

could tell it was the same man I'd spoken with the previous day.

"Let's go into my office and you can tell me how I may be of assistance."

Once they were in Bethany's office, the conversation would be even clearer and I knew they would be able to hear any movement I made, so I did my best to remain still as I listened through the vent. I could hear them arrange themselves into chairs before Bethany started her inquiry.

"My associate said you mentioned people were dying."

"Yes. And where is Mr. Galloway?"

Noise be damned. I reached into my desk drawer and withdrew a Sig Sauer P250 that a man with my history had no business possessing. In less than two seconds, I was in Bethany's office, the gun held behind my back. Across Bethany's desk sat a lean black man in khakis and an untucked blue button-down shirt. When he turned in the ancient chair we'd picked up at a secondhand store, I could see taut muscles in his forearms and the hint of strong biceps not quite covered by his sleeves.

The man's hands were empty, so I let my gaze move to Bethany. Her right hand had already drifted toward her own desk drawer where I knew she kept her Glock 43. For what seemed an eternity, nobody moved and nobody breathed. The man's eyes traced a line from my right shoulder down my arm to where it disappeared behind me, and he got the picture. He slowly swiveled his head to Bethany and noticed her hand was ominously out of sight as well. Like he was covered in rust, he raised his hands a few inches in the air.

"I think you have misjudged my intent," he said.

"I'm not officially listed as being part of the business," I said. "And I didn't tell you my name when we spoke. Who the hell are you?"

He lowered his hands onto the arms of the chair. Nothing in his expression indicated he was feeling anything but a detached coolness in the moment. Yes, he was being cautious, but the man was in a room with two people ready to fire bullets into his skull and his hands were steadier than a sedated sociopath playing Jenga. It was eighty-five degrees and humid outside and not a single bead of sweat had formed on the man's smooth head.

"I stated my name," he said with perfect calm. "You must have been listening if you heard me ask about you."

"I don't know you," I said.

Waterford nodded thoughtfully and didn't speak. Seconds passed and I looked at Bethany who cocked her head incredulously.

"Hey, buddy," she said. "Explain."

Waterford stopped his nodding and crossed his legs. "I may want to hire you. There is a delicate matter I need to discuss with you, and it requires absolute confidentiality."

Bethany brought her previously concealed hand to the top of the desk and slammed her Glock on the scratched-up oak surface.

"Why did you ask for Trevor?" she asked.

He nodded again, stopped, and said, "It seems I have raised some concerns on your end because I'm aware of Mr. Galloway's association with your business. Perhaps I should clarify."

"Perhaps," said Bethany, tapping her index finger on the gun.

"You are correct, Mr. Galloway, that you are not officially part of the business. You are not listed on the Business Tax Certificate or any other official documentation related to CCI. There is also no mention of you on the company website, and Ms. Nolan seems to have done well at keeping you…what's the phrase people in law enforcement say…off the grid."

I said, "Hardly anyone used that term until Jack Bauer did in the TV show *24*, but keep going."

Waterford held up a long finger. "However, you were listed on the lease for this building."

"The hell he was," said Bethany.

Waterford looked at me.

"Actually, I was," I said.

I remembered there was something at the end of the packet titled *Savannah Crime-Free House Program* that required all tenants to be listed. I remembered because I had lied on a question asking whether I'd ever been arrested. The form had six blank lines where I could explain my answer of "yes," but I didn't think six lines would cover it, and I didn't want Bethany to miss out on getting a spot for her business because of my past. I figured if the neighborhood was able to run any kind of criminal check it would be for active warrants only and I was golden on that account. However, since the landlord had already met me and knew I would be working in the building, I had to at least fill out the damn form.

"You were?" Bethany asked.

"He was," Waterford answered. "I am a thorough individual by nature, and I conducted extensive research on every private investigator in the area. While Ms. Nolan does not have a track record of which to speak," he turned to Bethany, "no offense. I used the internet to check up on Mr. Galloway." He turned his attention back to me and he said, "Your track record is significantly more…colorful."

If he was trying to put my mind at ease, he was failing miserably. I was already on high alert; now even more sirens were blaring in my head. I brought my gun around and held it down at my side.

"If you've read up on me, then there are only three reasons you could be here. One: this is a set-up and you're here to kill me or ID me for the people who would do the killing. Two: you read up on my…past…think I'm a hitter and you want somebody killed. Well, I don't do that. Three: you're out of your mind."

Although I added the third option, I knew he wasn't crazy. He was too cool—too collected. Also, he had somehow gotten hold of a form from a lease agreement, so his ability to organize thoughts and accumulate data was formidable.

"Mr. Galloway, if there is someone out there who wishes to do you harm, then this is the first I've heard of it."

He reached down toward his back pocket, and I raised the gun to my hip. Bethany gripped her Glock and pointed it at the man's chest. Waterford noted the movements and ignored them completely while he withdrew his wallet and pulled out a business card that he extended my way. Keeping my gun away from him so he couldn't possibly grab it, I accepted the card with my left hand and read the text.

"Google his name and the words 'Chatham County,'" I said to Bethany.

She placed her gun on the desk and turned to her laptop. After a few keystrokes and clicks of a mouse, she leaned back, reading from the monitor, "Sebastian Waterford. Chatham County—Board of Commissioners."

"Is there a photo?" I asked.

"Yes. It's him."

I lowered my gun but kept it at my side. I have trust issues.

"You have access to county records. That's how you know I'm not on the business license and how you got the document from the lease agreement."

"It is."

"Are you here on county business?" Bethany asked.

"Not officially."

"Then, I bet digging around in business and rental records for personal reasons could be construed as an abuse of power."

"It could," he said.

"But this doesn't worry you," I said, already knowing the answer.

"It's not a priority."

"What is the priority?" I asked.

"Have you read about the 9-1-1 killings?"

Bethany and I nodded. It had been all over the news. Family members of four dispatchers had been murdered, and the killer had called 9-1-1 at 9:11 PM on various nights over the past few months. The emergency response system was in a crisis, as poorly paid communication officers were quitting or calling in sick because they were afraid their loved ones could be the next victims.

"I need you to find the killer," Waterford said.

Bethany slid open her desk drawer and put her gun away. She leaned back in her chair and crossed her arms.

She said, "You have several police departments at your disposal, and I'm sure the feds have already offered to assist. Even if you *did* want to farm this out to the private sector, there are several large investigative firms with unlimited resources that would take this on in a heartbeat. Yet, you want to hire an agency run by someone that—as you so insightfully mentioned—has no track record—and whose lone, unofficial employee is *colorful*. I know this isn't much of a sales pitch," she said, "but why come to us?"

Waterford uncrossed his legs and leaned forward in the chair, folding his hands in front of him. "Large firms like headlines and are filled with former police officers and retired federal agents who talk to current police officers and current federal agents. This investigation would be strictly off-the-books. The county would not be paying for your services. I would be writing the checks. I assume your rate is reasonable and media coverage is not something you desire since it seems you are keeping Mr. Galloway in the shadows."

I tucked my gun into the back of my jeans and slid his business card into my pocket.

"You think it's an inside job," I said. "That's why you're concerned about former cops talking to current cops."

"Someone is getting the personal information of these communication officers. The last killing wasn't the dispatcher's husband or wife. It was the girl's grandmother and her two cousins who happened to be living there while a family dispute was being settled. The grandmother's address was on the girl's initial job application from when she had to list places she'd lived in the past. The killer avoided hitting a primary family member that the police might be watching and went to a softer target." For the first time, a hint of emotion crept onto his face. "This widens the pool of potential victims, and then there is always the possibility the pendulum will swing the other way and the killer will move away from secondary family members and toward the dispatchers themselves."

"You don't talk like a politician," Bethany said.

Waterford stood and the brief flash of emotion he displayed was gone. "Are you interested in the job?"

"You don't want former cops involved," I said. "But I'm a former cop."

A corner of Waterford's mouth crept up. "I could be mistaken," he said, "but judging from the stories I've read, I'm guessing you have been largely excommunicated from the law enforcement community."

I still had Chase, but Waterford wasn't wrong.

"Do you want the job?" he asked again.

My eyes met Bethany's and, like always, I knew we were on the same page. We'd tell Waterford we needed to discuss things in private and would get back to him in a day or two. No need to rush into things. Taking on a case like this was a big decision. If somehow our involvement became public, it was possible my name could get thrown around and it could harm her fledgling business. Also, we had no idea what kind of fee to charge for a case like this. If we were to take it on, we had to decide on a fair rate and estimate our expenses. There was a lot to consider.

"Absolutely," she said.

Yep. Totally on the same page.

Chapter 4

Trevor Galloway

The house we were renting was in a part of town near Grayson Stadium. While the house was in better condition than the office, we weren't exactly living in luxury. However, we'd thrown in an extra thousand with our security deposit and worked out a deal with the owner who didn't ask questions as we made several upgrades to the two-story Italianate-style home. The wooden doors were gone, replaced with steel versions while reinforcing the frames so our entryways could withstand anything short of a wrecking ball. We'd also had a state-of-the-art alarm system installed as well as a camera system we could monitor from our cell phones. There was also an assortment of weapons secreted throughout the house, should the need arise for us to mount a defense. While all the precautions might have seemed like overkill to most people, they were reasonable under the circumstances.

Back when I was a narcotics detective, I'd been taken captive by a drug gang and turned into little more than a zombie addict. While I'd love to say I was a pillar of strength, throughout the weeks of torture and days I'd been kept high, I had divulged valuable operational details regarding ongoing investigations as well as the identities of several informants. Two of those confidential informants ended up dead. In fact, the detective who was running one of those informants was none other than Erik Draymon. The fact I'd hunted down the ringleader and killed him in what may, or may not, have been a good shooting hadn't improved my standing with Draymon or anyone else in the department. Ultimately, I was forced into taking a disability retirement. From the scene at the wedding, it was apparent Draymond's opinion of me hadn't softened, and I knew many others felt the same way. My reputation in Pittsburgh didn't improve after I became entangled in a case, lost someone close to me, and exacted revenge on those responsible, leaving a trail of blood throughout the city. I'd been extremely lucky to have only spent two years in a mental institution for my crimes, and if people knew I was now totally off my meds, they would clamor for my immediate incarceration. The meds made my hallucinations go away but clouded my mind to the point of making me useless. Anyway, as of late, it seemed there might be some light at the end of that tunnel.

"Any ideas for dinner?" I asked from the living room.

"Whatever you're making," was the response from the bedroom.

A few moments later, Bethany emerged wearing jeans and an Imagine Dragons shirt. Not my favorite band, but the tight shirt looked good on her.

"I can whip up a stir-fry."

"That's fine," she said as she moved over to the narrow table beside the front door and began thumbing through the few days of mail that had accumulated while we'd been out of town.

As yet another precaution, we didn't use the house as our mailing address. Instead, we had a P.O. Box and we'd stopped and gotten our mail on the way home from the office. Bethany had been uncharacteristically distant since Chase's wedding, and I was determined not to push. Normally she could be counted on to remain level, but in a matter of minutes, she'd gone from pushing for an engagement to pushing me away. Well, if anyone could wait her out, it was me. They didn't call me the Tin Man because of my inability to control my emotions. Other than those few times when I had *really* lost it, I was good at playing the waiting game.

We sat at our breakfast table, which doubled as our dinner table, as we ate my mediocre chicken stir-fry and drank a merlot we picked up from the Whole Foods down the street. We made small talk and heard the muffled sound of sirens from Fire Station #8. The noise from the firetrucks could be annoying, but moving in close to a fire station had been a strategic decision on our part. It wouldn't do any good to place ourselves inside a fortress if the enemy could simply burn the place to the ground. While we couldn't account for every variable, we had to play the odds the best we could, and being in close proximity to a fire station seemed like a good enough idea.

"Is it okay?" I asked.

"I'm fine," she answered absently.

"No," I said. "The food. Is it okay?"

She looked up. "Oh. It's good. Thanks for cooking."

"We should talk about the case," I suggested.

She put down her fork and brushed a strand of hair away from her forehead.

"You think we should have talked about it before I accepted the case."

I did, but that ship had sailed, and I didn't see any point in dwelling on the decision. The fee Bethany had negotiated seemed fair, but what did I know?

I shook my head and said, "It's your company. It's your call."

"It's my name on some documents, but you know I consider it *our* business. Without you—"

"Anybody can conduct routine surveillance," I said. "I know I'm not adding value to this venture."

She said, "I've seen what you're capable of, and divorce cases aren't giving you the opportunity to use your talents."

"They're safe," I reminded her.

"They're boring."

"Hasn't *boring* been an unexpected gift?" I asked.

At the conclusion of my last case, a man named Mr. Simon, a shady fixer for a one-time presidential candidate, had let the members of the EEDC know I was in Savannah. As a courtesy, Mr. Simon had sent me a video in which I could see him hand a representative of the drug gang a photo of Bethany and me walking down River Street. We'd assumed it would be weeks or possibly a couple of months until one or two of their enforcers showed up with guns blazing. Amazingly, a year had passed and nothing had transpired. I was hoping—I was praying—the gang was under new management and had decided to forget about me. Over the past few years, I'd ended up taking out a few of their guys, and maybe they'd decided the cost of chasing one broken-down detective wasn't worth the risk.

"We still have our savings from Pittsburgh, but it won't last forever," said Bethany. "We need real cases."

I sipped my wine and nodded. She wasn't wrong, but there were several things nagging at me. Sebastian Waterford was one of them. He had the job title of a politician but the demeanor and awareness of something else. If we were moving forward with this investigation, I'd have to know more about our client. Aside from the enigma of Waterford, there was a bigger elephant in the room and Bethany knew it.

"Do you want to start taking your meds again? Low doses? Just in case?"

I shook my head. "You know I can't. Do you want me to go back to being pale, skeletal, and unable to form a coherent thought?"

"You haven't seen any of them in months. Not even Lukas."

My stomach turned. *Fucking Lukas.*

Most of the time the bastard wants me dead and then every once in a while he seems to want to help me out. I thought maybe we'd come to an understanding, but now he'd melted away like a puff of smoke on a windy day. While I should have considered his absence a blessing, something told me he was still out there watching and waiting.

"I know," I said. "I want to keep it that way."

"So, we do this," she began. "You handle the grunt work and come out with me for face-to-face interactions as much as you feel comfortable. However, consider yourself a consultant. This is not *your* case. You have no emotional investment in this investigation. I'm using you for your mental resources only. You're essentially a computer program I may want to access from time to time. You're nothing but software."

"Stop. I'm blushing."

"I'm serious. You have a habit of getting too wrapped up in cases, and that can't happen here. You'll be involved peripherally, but you absolutely...positively...can't get to the point you're doing your—"

"No blur-outs," I said.

"Right. Because you are a detached, objective consultant. A reference book I can pick up off the shelf."

"Is this foreplay?" I asked. "Because it feels like foreplay."

Her expression let me know it wasn't foreplay.

Bethany said, "If your hallucinations are truly the result of PTSD and all that happened to you before, then we'll do our best to keep the stress out of our lives."

If? What did that mean? That's been the diagnosis for years. I told myself I was reading too much into her choice of words and to let it go.

"Okay, boss. What's the first move?"

"I'll set up a meeting with Waterford and have him provide me with background on each of the dispatchers who had family members killed. You see what you can find out about our client. He's obviously not your average political hack, and I want to make sure we're not being played here."

"Okay."

She looked like she wanted to say something else, but stopped. I started to prompt her but didn't. We sipped more merlot. In the distance, the sirens from Station #8 wound up once again.

Chapter 5

Trevor Galloway

Bethany was already out the door when I awoke the next morning. I ate some toast and downed a cup of coffee before sauntering over to our makeshift gym. With having expected EEDC enforcers to descend on Savannah, we'd forgone getting a typical gym membership, as the mental image of me being relatively defenseless in a public place while suspending a heavy barbell above my chest wasn't particularly appealing. As an alternative, we'd hit Craigslist and picked up a decent amount of used exercise equipment that we squeezed into a spare room on the second floor. After years of living in Pennsylvania, my instinct was to turn the basement into a gym, but it seemed living at sea level meant basements weren't really a *thing* on the Georgia coast.

This was my back and shoulder day, which I liked a lot less than my chest and arm routine, but infinitely more than leg day. I powered up the Bluetooth speaker I'd mounted on the wall, and it automatically connected to my phone. Since Bethany wasn't home to complain about my choice in music, I found Mötley Crüe's Greatest Hits album on my playlist and shuffled the order of songs, and the recognizable heavy intro of *Dr. Feelgood* shook the room. After stretching, I used my bench and free weights to crank out several sets of dumbbell rows followed by sets of shoulder presses. I performed a shoulder fly routine and then knocked out some crunches for good measure. The whole routine took me less than forty-five minutes but helped keep my body and mind in tune.

Although I was going to be working from home, I prepared myself as if I were going to into an office as had become my routine since we'd moved south. For whatever reason, when I dressed as if I was going into work, some mental switch flipped and it helped me focus. It seemed I wasn't one of those people who could sit and work while in the pajamas, so I put on a pair of jeans and a golf shirt. It wasn't exactly business attire, but it made me feel better that I didn't look like a hobo.

My first-floor home office was little more than a desk, a squeaky chair, a laptop, a printer I rarely used, and four walls in need of a fresh coat of paint. I'd hung a couple of framed movie posters on the walls, mostly because I knew people do that sort of thing. On the wall behind my chair was a promotional shot for the film *Heat*—Robert De Niro, Al Pacino, and Val Kilmer gazing out with varying levels of intensity. Daniel Craig appraised my working space from the opposite wall as he stepped out of *Casino Royale*, suppressed pistol in hand.

Taking Bethany's advice, I fired up the laptop and began the stress-free task of digging into the background of Sebastian Waterford. I began by running a search for the Chatham County Board of Commissioners. The first search result was a link that took me directly to a page consisting of the nine members of the Board. I found Waterford's name and photo and clicked on the box for *6th District*.

Born in Macon, Georgia, Sebastian McAliman Waterford had earned a bachelor's degree in economics from Winthrop University and a master of public administration from the College of Charleston after serving several years in the U.S. Air Force. He served as the Chief of Staff for the Mayor of Augusta, Georgia before eventually settling in Savannah to work with disadvantaged youths. A proud member of the NAACP, Waterford was elected to the Commission at the conclusion of the most recent election and was expected to serve a four-year term. I scrolled down the page to see more, but that was all there was to see. No information about family or any specific details about his military service. Curious, I checked out the bios of the other board members and each of them was significantly more extensive, reading like a resume for future aspirations rather than an obligation to be fulfilled for the current position.

After trying my luck and failing at finding more information about Waterford on the Chatham County site, I decided to run a simple internet search of his name to see where that would take me. With a name like *Sebastian McAliman Waterford*, I knew I wasn't likely to get a lot of duplicate hits, and I was right. I immediately found links connected to Waterford's work in Augusta. The links led me to innocuous press releases and other public statements about tax increases, garbage collection rates, a scandal involving a city official who got her boyfriend a low-level job in the government, and various other municipal business matters.

Opening and closing a few more pages didn't yield anything particularly useful, but I did eventually find a write-up about the man in a magazine called *Augusta Monthly*. The piece appeared to be part of an ongoing series titled "Next Up," focusing on people and places that were expected to be the "next big thing" in the Augusta area. The focus of that month's article was none other than the Mayor's Chief of Staff. Beside a narrow column of text was an image of a purposeful Waterford, carrying a thick folder under one arm while striding out of an official-looking building. The candid shot caught the man in mid-step, his azure tie flapping to the side of his fat-free torso, as sunlight reflected off his cobalt suit.

The author of the column described Waterford as the "strategic mastermind" behind the mayor's successful bid for reelection the previous year and a "much-needed calming presence" in an administration that had ruled by emotion in previous years. The article went on to note that since the current mayor had no intention of running for a third term, it was nearly a certainty Waterford would step in as his party's candidate and would be a heavy favorite to be the next chief executive of the city. A line of text in small font followed the column. It read, "Sebastian Waterford declined to be interviewed for this column." I went back and read the entire piece more carefully. In the vaguest sense, the columnist had sketched out Waterford's biographical information, but it contained little more information than had the Chatham County government page.

I closed the page that contained the *Augusta Monthly* article and searched for news articles related to the mayoral race in which Waterford would have been a candidate. When I found one, I discovered several candidates had thrown their hats in the ring for the big seat, but none of them was Sebastian Waterford. In fact, I couldn't find any articles whatsoever about his exit from the Augusta political scene.

My chair groaned as I swiveled it in the direction of the window that faced E. 48th Street. The occasional car passed by and dog walkers tug on leashes as I contemplated our new client. Whatever had been pinging on my sonar regarding Waterford was only getting louder. Thus far, Waterford's life had gaps, and a politician with gaps can be a dangerous animal. But he didn't *act* like a politician. Who enters the political arena, ultimately runs for election as a county commissioner, but seems to shun the spotlight as much as possible?

Gaps.

The stress-free activity of basic research became more stressful as I thought about Bethany meeting with the man with an uncertain history who was hiring us off-the-books. Part of me knew I should have gone with her. She could take care of herself, that was for certain. However, I knew *we* could take care of ourselves even better.

My train of thought ran afoul when I noticed a glint of

movement at the edge of the window. I rose from my seat, leaned close to the glass, and thought I caught a glimpse of the back of someone's dark shirt going toward the front of the house. In less than two seconds, I'd retrieved a H&K 9mm from my desk drawer and was moving through the first floor. Bethany had certainly set the alarm upon leaving in the morning, but I swept the rooms as I made my way toward the back as a precaution. In my sock-covered feet, I padded softly toward the rear door, knowing that in this part of the home, I couldn't be seen from the outside. Sunlight seeped through the edges of the windows on either side of the door, but each of them was covered with shades. Suddenly, I caught sight of a shadow crossing the window to the right of the door. I trained my sights on the door and waited. Ten seconds passed. Nothing. Twenty seconds. Nothing. No shadows passed by the other window, indicating either the person had stopped at the door and was waiting, had backed away, or had ducked down under the windows.

Slowly, I knelt on one knee and waited another two minutes. Finally, I rose and crept over to the left window and peeked behind the blinds. I saw no one. Cautiously, I moved from window to window, checking each available vantage point. No threats. At some point, I became aware there was an armed crazy man in socks prowling around my house and peering out the windows, and I felt ridiculous instantly.

I went to the alarm panel near the front door and disarmed it. After taking another paranoid look out a front window, I tucked the gun into the back of my pants and opened the front door. Several houses down the block, I saw a man with a dark shirt dart toward the front door of a house and then return to the sidewalk. Then he repeated the exercise at the next house. He did the same thing again, and again, and again. Delivering the mail, just like his employers at the U.S. Postal Service expected him to.

The disadvantage of living on a corner lot is that people, like postal workers, might be tempted to take a quick shortcut through your yard. *Still...why go from the front to the back?* I moved around the house and followed the same path as the shadow I'd seen. There was no chance of seeing any footprints in the dry centipede grass that was prominent along the Georgia coast. Nothing had been disturbed on the back door itself. However, a patch of mulch beside the concrete square adjacent to the door had been disturbed, and brown flecks of bark had been kicked up out of the mulch bed.

Of course, it had been a few days since I'd been in the backyard, so the disturbance could have been caused anytime by a squirrel...or a cat. Or a confused postal worker...who would have had no reason to be that close to the back porch.

Perspective, Galloway. Keep it all in perspective, I told myself. A handful of mulch does not a killer drug gang make.

I did my best to shake off my rivaling feelings of reasonable awareness and ridiculous paranoia, so I could get back to my research. Just because Sebastian Waterford didn't advertise parts of his life didn't mean there wasn't a little mulch to dig up. I'd just dive in a little.

Chapter 6

Bethany Nolan

I'd arrived at the coffee shop on Liberty Street well before Waterford was scheduled to arrive. I told myself I wanted to have time to wake up and get my thoughts together before our meeting, but the truth was I wanted to get out of the house before Trevor awoke. There was something hanging between us now—a heavy curtain keeping us in earshot of one another, but not quite together. *Soon*, was what I'd mouthed to Trevor, feeling a pang of regret the moment it had happened. Seeing Chase and Lauren standing at the front of the church, preparing to take their vows, I did something I never do. I got a little carried away. Not that I don't *want* to marry Trevor. I do. But, then there's the *other* thing.

Students shuffled in and out, getting their caffeine fixes before heading to classes at the Savannah College of Art and Design. The colorful array of punk, goth, emo, and run-of-the-mill flamboyant SCAD kids contrasted beautifully with city streets that still saw their share of horse-drawn carriages. Of course, here I was calling them *kids*. Part of me didn't feel any more grown-up than any of the nineteen-year-olds with ten piercings, who were wearing T-shirts of bands that had stopped playing years before they drank their first bottle of milk, much less had a latte.

What the hell was I doing here? A year ago, I was in Pittsburgh and, while my life wasn't ideal, I felt I belonged. The rivers and countless bridges stretched out like a Vitruvian Man and connected people who, yes, had problems and complaints but seemed to commiserate together about the ailments of the stretched-out body. Savannah, with its fascinating but schizophrenic history of war, slavery, resilience, survival, wealth, poverty, hospitality, and protectiveness was a city I had yet to understand. And the gnats in Savannah bite. Literally, they *bite*. What was God thinking with that one?

Feeling lost was wearing on me, and for the first time in my life, I was starting to feel sorry for myself—which *really* pissed me off. I didn't want to admit it, but I was a novice investigator and CCI was looking like it was becoming a failure. While I did my best to project confidence, there were realities I had to face. I was in love with a man who, in addition to being a mentally unbalanced killer and the target of a small cartel, was too old for me. Now, here I was debating having a third cup of coffee while waiting to talk to a client who came to me only because Trevor and I haven't been successful enough for anyone to take note. At least the coffee was good.

As I had done when going to get my second coffee, I left my notebook and pen on the reclaimed-wood table, so as to announce my seat was taken. Rarely did I carry cash, so I reached down into the pocket of my capris to get my credit card. Instinctively, I glanced down, as if my pocket might have relocated itself in the past twenty minutes. I'd only made it a step or two before Sebastian Waterford, wearing a salmon button-down shirt and gray slacks, appeared in front of me. *Jesus*. I considered myself an observant individual, but he'd somehow entered the shop, slid through a sea of mostly white kids shorter than him, and walked right up to me before I'd finished reaching in my pocket. He extended his hand, and we shook.

"Ms. Nolan, it is good to see you again."

"You can call me Bethany," I said.

"You don't go by Beth?"

I nearly cringed at hearing the name. "It never took," I said.

"Please call me Sebastian."

"No nicknames?"

"They never took," he said with a slight grin.

He released my hand and said, "Were you getting another coffee? Let me get it for you."

"No," I said. "I've probably had enough anyway."

"Well, I would like something," he said. "If you don't mind, I'll get myself a drink, and then we can talk. Will Mr. Galloway be joining us?"

I shook my head. "He's tied up on something else at the moment."

"Okay. I'll be back in a minute," he told me as he headed to the counter.

As he walked away, something about his stride caught my notice. His gait seemed off when he worked his way around some of the other customers. When he tried to make a right turn, he limped badly, but then he seemed to correct it. As athletic as he appeared, I assumed he might be the *get up and run five miles before dawn* type, so a sore muscle or two would be understandable. By the time he'd returned, I was in my seat, notebook and pen at the ready. While Trevor and I had done some preliminary research online, I wanted to hear about the 9-1-1 killings from Waterford himself since I assumed he could lend more insight than the Savannah Morning News.

"Where should we begin?" he asked as he settled in and took a drink from a cup of orange juice.

"I figured you for a black coffee type of guy," I said, jotting down the date in my notebook.

"No. I can't stand coffee. I don't even like the smell."

I looked up. "It was your idea to meet in this coffee shop," I reminded him.

"Yes," he said. "It's best if we don't meet in my office, and nobody knows me here."

"You're a public figure," I said. "You're recognizable."

"Ninety percent of people in this county have no idea what their county commissioner looks like, and the other ten percent are probably mistaken," he said.

I smiled. He had a point. I didn't have a clue what district of the county Trevor and I lived in, much less who represented us.

"We could have met in my office," I said.

"True. However, although I'm not usually recognized in public, if I'm seen going into a private investigator's office once, then I can explain it away. If I'm seen there twice, matters could be more complicated. I don't know if I'll run for another term or not, but I'd prefer to not hand any potential opponents even the hint of a scandal."

"Is that all?" I said, suspiciously.

"No," he said, taking a sip of juice.

I waited.

"Your office smells like mold."

Again...he had a fair point.

I scooted my chair away from the table and held my notebook in my lap.

"Okay. Tell me about the murders."

Waterford leaned forward, letting his elbows rest on the worn planks of the table while both his hands enveloped his drink. He took in a breath and began.

"It started five months ago, on December 12th. By all accounts, it was a typical weeknight; there were no special events, no unusual gang activity, nothing major going on in the city or out in the county. The calls into the communications center were the usual vehicle accidents, fistfights, and disturbance calls. The city had been on a two-week stretch of no homicides, which seems pretty good these days. There had been a slight uptick on shoplifting calls, with the stores being busy for the holiday season, but nothing of significance. Marcus Hauke, a communications officer with six years of experience, answered a call at 9:11 PM. The caller ID was blocked and was from an unknown location."

Waterford's right hand dropped beneath the table; he shifted his weight and produced a small digital recorder with a set of earbuds attached and wound around the device. He uncoiled the cord for the earbuds from around the recorder and offered one to me while placing the other in his ear. Once I was set, he played the recording.

The first speaker had a thick southern drawl and conveyed an easygoing manner.

Chatham 9-1-1. What's your emergency?

The second voice sounded deep and electronically distorted.

Emergency?

Yes, sir. You sound a bit garbled. Do you have an emergency?

No, no. Haley has an emergency.

Okay. Who is Haley, and what is her emergency?

There was a pause.

Sir, are you still there?

Yes. Is Haley?

Is Haley what, sir?

The easygoing tone of Hauke's voice was gone and a trace of irritation was seeping through. Still, he remained professional. The distorted voice continued.

Is Haley there?

Sir, who is Haley, and what is the emergency?

I'm sure you know Haley. She must be sitting near you right now. Have you met her fiancé?

Another pause ensued, this one longer than the previous. When Hauke did speak, it was clear the "good ol' boy" calmness that was probably his trademark had left the building.

Sir, where are you calling from?

The caller answered in a sing-song manner.

Ted is waiting. He can't wait long. You better tell the police to run along.

Waterford pressed a button on the recorder, and we removed our earbuds.

Referring to the research I had already done, I said, "The

Haley mentioned is Haley Stringer. Her fiancé, Ted Whittle, was found dead in his garage."

"That's one way to put it," said Waterford.

"What's another way?"

Waterford leaned in. "His body was found ablaze in his garage. The killer tied him to a chair, poured a can of gasoline over him, and lit him up."

"I don't remember reading that in the media reports," I said. "Most simply stated the body of Ted Whittle had been burned."

"The police didn't know what they had on their hands, so they made sure to keep as many details as they could out of the media."

Waterford's mention of the police brought a question to mind. While Trevor and I had been in Savannah for a while, I was still confused about jurisdictional lines.

"Most of the reports I read gave Ted Whittle's address as Savannah, but I saw statements were given by the Chatham County Police Department. And sometimes I see police cars that have the words *Savannah-Chatham Police* down the side. Is there one department for Savannah and the surrounding county?"

Waterford put the recorder on the table and rubbed his head as if I'd asked him to decipher the Rosetta Stone.

"You have to remember I've only been here a few years too, so it was confusing to me as well. The short version is there's a Savannah PD *and* a Chatham County PD. The slightly longer version is the two departments merged a few years ago, the merger didn't work out, and they split again. However, there are still some cars out there that bear the *Savannah-Chatham* label. The whole thing was a huge mess."

"Why didn't the merger work out?"

"An assortment of reasons. One of the primary ones was response times. That's always a hot-button issue, but what can you expect when tens of thousands of people live along narrow roads that cross countless intercostal waterways. Combine all of that with tidal flooding, severe storms, hurricanes, tornadoes, and all that goes along with the changing climate so many southern politicians want to deny, and it's a first-responder nightmare."

"Remind me, where was Ted Whittle killed?"

"Whitemarsh Island, in a subdivision off Johnny Mercer Boulevard. It's just outside the city limits."

"I'd like to see the police report and any follow-up investigative reports," I said.

"I can get those to you."

"Are they insightful?"

"They are detailed. The investigators noted there were signs of forced entry. Also, the coroner found evidence of a subdural hematoma, indicating it is possible Whittle had been struck on the head in order to subdue him. As far as anything else forensically on the body, it's likely the fire took care of that. I assume that is the type of information you're looking for?"

"For starters. I also want to know if the killer brought the gas can with him or if it was already in Whittle's garage."

"I don't recall, but I'm sure it's in the reports. CCPD is terribly understaffed, but they know what they're doing."

I didn't say anything for a long moment.

"What?" asked Waterford.

"Do you think he was already dead? Do you think the killer was lying and Whittle was dead before the 9-1-1 call was ever made?"

Waterford's gaze lowered to the table. "No. He was alive when the call was made."

"How can you be sure?"

Waterford seemed to consider something and then offered one of the earbuds to me once again. I placed it in my ear. He didn't do the same. Waterford took a long second before pressing play. I wish to God he hadn't.

Chapter 7

Bethany Nolan

I excused myself to get a coffee I didn't want. Waterford had put the recorder away by the time I'd returned to our table.

"I shouldn't have let you hear—"

"It's okay," I replied while taking my seat. "That's part of the job."

The recording had been difficult to listen to, but I wasn't going to show that to a client. I needed to keep things moving along. Knowing Trevor, he'd probably gotten out of bed, blasted his ridiculous eighties music while working out, and then dove straight into learning more about our client. While I wasn't expecting him to be heavily involved in the case, I certainly wanted to go back with more information than Trevor would have uncovered.

"Tell me about the second killing," I said.

"That call came in nearly four weeks later. No progress had been made in the Whittle homicide investigation, and there was no reason to believe it wasn't an isolated, targeted occurrence."

Waterford's mind seemed to drift off somewhere. Perhaps he was recalling the emotions of realizing what exactly they had on their hands.

"Until—" I prompted.

"Until the call came in at exactly eleven minutes after nine on January 15th. I have the recording of that call as well…I have all of them. They're all on here."

He produced a flash drive and slid it across the table.

"The call was much like the first. An inexperienced dispatcher named Jamie Byrum took the call. She answered the call in the usual way; the caller stated, '*You* have an emergency.' He then went on to ask Ms. Byrum if she knew Eric Daughtry."

"I read he was one of the communications officers on duty at the time," I said.

Waterford nodded. "Byrum hadn't been on duty when the December call had come in, but despite her inexperience, she realized what was happening. She signaled for the shift supervisor to come over to her station and listen in on the call. However, all the caller did after that was give the address of Eric Daughtry's residence before saying, 'Run, run as fast as you can. You might save her. But I doubt that you can.'"

"How was his wife killed?" I asked. "I mean, I read what was in the news, but what wasn't released to the public?"

"There wasn't anything to withhold for that one. It was manual strangulation, plain and simple. He, and I realize I'm assuming it was a *he*, seemed to have gained access through the back door and used his bare hands to end Marleen Daughtry's life. At least, we're guessing he used the back door since it was left open and the front door was locked."

I took a sip of my coffee. It was cold. "Interesting," I said.

"How so?"

I hesitated. I wasn't sure why. "Nothing. I'm just thinking out loud. Who responded to the call?"

"That one was in the city limits, so Savannah PD has jurisdiction."

"I'm assuming there is a joint task force?"

Waterford smiled, started to speak, but stopped himself.

"What is it?"

"Forgive me," he said. "I was about to say something that

would have come across as condescending."

"Well, now you *have* to say it."

"I was going to say that for a young person with relatively little experience in this world, you seem to have figured out how organizations handle these types of investigations. I mean no offense."

"I'll take it as a compliment," I said, meaning it.

"To answer your question, yes, there is a task force now. It not only includes investigators from CCPD and Savannah PD, but also some of the smaller incorporated jurisdictions scattered in and around the county. Those jurisdictions were included in the interest of information sharing and to ensure there weren't any bureaucratic hurdles when questioning suspects, talking to witnesses, or conducting surveillance."

"Has that been helpful thus far?" I asked.

"Has what been helpful?"

"Any of it. The task force, including the smaller departments, all of the collaboration."

Waterford didn't take long to think about his response. "No. But, not for lack of expertise or effort. There simply have not been any suspects to question, no witnesses to speak of, and the only surveillance conducted was on a few individuals who had a history of making threats against police officers or city officials. It was a pure fishing expedition and, as expected, nothing panned out."

"Okay. What about the third murder? That was the one at the business, right?"

"Yes. That was the only one not committed in a home or apartment. Taylor LaFreniere was working late, doing inventory at her small bookstore downtown. Her husband had the bad fortune of taking the call at the communications center that night. This was only two weeks since Marleen Daughtry had been strangled, so he knew what was happening the moment the distorted voice came through his headset. This time, the caller simply gave the address and said something like, 'A page here, a chapter there. Rush, rush, or you'll find her everywhere.'"

Something in Waterford's expression darkened as he conveyed the sickeningly playful words of the killer who I knew then went on to slit LaFreniere's throat and cut off her hands with a boning saw found at the scene.

The politician shifted uncomfortably as he described the scene. I took notes and reminded myself to later make sure everything matched up with the investigative reports.

"He cut the hands off at the wrists, because it seems...easily cutting through bone with a saw is more of a Hollywood thing. With a tool like that, one really has to get through the joints, because you can...anyway, it's easier," Waterford informed me as he finished giving me the gruesome details I didn't really want to hear but needed to verify against the reports.

"The most recent attack was two weeks ago. Alicia Montez lost her grandmother and two cousins. These were the only killings that involved a gun. Alicia said her grandmother always kept the door locked, and there were no signs of forced entry. The working theory is the killer simply knocked on the door and then forced his way in. Officers canvassed the apartment complex and took statements, and there were a few people who thought they might have heard gunshots. One man said he heard three shots at 9:15 PM. If that's accurate, and the killer really was in the apartment when he called, then he killed all three victims four minutes after calling dispatch."

"That's quite a gamble," I said.

"It's more than that. It could be recklessness, but I don't think that's the case. I think this is an indication that when this individual has a mission with a determined set of parameters, he isn't going to deviate, no matter what hell is about to rain down. He's going to stay on target and assume certain risks." Waterford began speaking with more fire. "If that's the case, this person is calculating, relentless, and won't stop until he is caught."

I waited to see if Waterford was finished. He became self-conscious, as people do when they are accustomed to being measured in their words.

"We have six victims thus far and no suspects. There are some outstanding investigators in the police departments here, but I fear something is going to get missed in the tangle of bureaucracies. I'm assuming the feds will join the investigation soon, but I'm not certain that will help matters. And as Mr. Galloway deduced, I have my suspicions the killer either works for the county or is otherwise getting information from county employment records. Therefore, I don't know who to trust, and I'm keeping this investigation off the books. If asked about the identity of your client, I would suggest you lie and say you were retained by a member of one of the victim's family members but cannot disclose which one."

I thought for a moment before asking, "Why you?"

"What do you mean?"

"Why are *you* coming to us? The Board of Commissioners has what, nine members? Between Savannah PD, Chatham County PD, and all the rest, there have got to be dozens of experienced law enforcement officials looking at this from every angle. Yet, it's you that's taking the initiative to finance a private investigation."

"Someone else could be doing the same but using another P.I."

"You're dodging the question, Commissioner."

He smiled at that and after a pause said, "I hate injustice. And while I obviously believe in government service, I've seen public institutions fail to achieve justice too many times. Sometimes the failures have been caused by individual egos, other times it was simply a matter of overly complicated rules and regulations that nobody could follow. Regardless, I like to cover all contingencies and leave nothing to chance."

"Is that all?" I asked, suspecting it wasn't.

Waterford considered my question. "I'm always thinking about the Bystander Effect."

"What's that?"

"I'm certain you know what it is, even if you've never heard it given that specific name. The most infamous example occurred in

Queens, New York. In 1964, a woman named Kitty Genovese was stabbed and sexually assaulted while walking home from work. She died from the attack. Thirty-eight people witnessed the attack. Do you know how many intervened? How many called the police during the attack? Zero. Not one."

"Everyone assumed someone else would step up," I said solemnly. "I've heard of several similar examples."

Waterford nodded and then looked me in the eyes. "I'm not going to be a bystander wearing a permanent badge of regret." He tapped a finger on the table with each of his next words. "It's not going to happen."

I asked Waterford to contact me whenever he had the investigative files and told him he could email them to me if he felt comfortable doing so. We shook hands, and he left before me. I sat for another ten minutes thinking about the case and probably avoiding the tense situation at home with Trevor. I just needed to focus on the case and then deal with the domestic situation. Of course, part of me was concerned Trevor might go down one of his dark mental alleyways, but I was pretty proud of the way I'd convinced him to stay at home and do light research on Waterford. At least with Trevor doing nothing more than Googling and drinking coffee, I could rest assured he wasn't going off the deep end.

Chapter 8

Bethany Nolan

"What the fuck?" I yelled.

"Come look at this."

"I can see it from here!" I said from the doorway of the thrift store–IKEA mash-up Trevor referred to as his home office.

Some of Trevor's eighties music was playing from a Bluetooth speaker in the corner. Poison, I think. Or maybe that was Ratt. Trevor's hair was in disarray, and streaks of red and orange ran down his arms. There were open packs of markers we hadn't owned previously sitting on the desk, and the air smelled of fresh ink. A gun was on the desk. He gestured to the wall, admired his work, and then looked at me expectantly. My mouth fell open as I surveyed the disorder.

We'd never gotten around to painting any of the rooms, and most of the walls, including those in the home office, had been a shade of off-white. Trevor had removed a movie poster from one of the walls, which was now multicolored, and had drawn something akin to a colorful jigsaw puzzle with numbered pieces. The irregular shapes Trevor had filled in appeared to be randomly fractured by areas he hadn't touched, looking like white blood vessels stretched across the wall from right to left with many originating with wide mouths and narrowing until they terminated somewhere in the center. Some branches connected to create an interwoven pattern that could only be described as frantic.

"What have you done?" I asked with my mouth agape.

He looked at me as if the answer to my question should have been obvious.

Trevor said, "Our man Sebastian is a tough nut to crack. I hope you got some background on him because I'm going to need a little more time to get a read on the guy. I've got some calls out to a few people, but in the meantime, I started working on this."

He walked up to his creation and pointed to a purple dot located in one of the shapes. That particular shape was colored red, and now I noticed it had the number four in the center. In fact, although there weren't purple dots in each outlined area, each one had a number.

"Trevor..."

He turned toward the wall and said, "Here's what doesn't make sense."

"Trevor, stop."

"If you look at the dots I've made—"

"Stop!"

He pivoted around with a concerned expression on his face. Using his cell phone, he turned off the music.

"You have to stop."

"I...this is just—"

"A map. It's a district map of Chatham County. Eight districts, the white space are waterways, different colors for different districts, purple dots for the sites of the homicides. I get it."

"You do? Great. I thought it might be too messy to—"

"Background on Sebastian Waterford. That's what you were supposed to be doing. Low-key, calm, background research."

"I was. I mean, I did. He was a popular staffer for the mayor in Augusta after getting out of the military. From what I can tell, he was all but certain to become the next mayor but pulled up stakes and moved here. It's weird." He rushed over to his computer and spun the monitor in my direction, nearly tipping it over. "And there are gaps here and there, but not in a consistent way. It's like...well, no, that doesn't make sense. I need more information. I hit a dead end for the moment, so I started looking at the locations where the killer struck. And if there are more murders, this map will come in handy because we'll have—"

"You're high."

He looked offended.

"You know I'm not. I haven't touched anything stronger than a Tylenol since we met."

"Not that kind of high. Casework high. You're buzzed on the chase, and we're just getting started. You can't do this. We both know where this leads. I've heard about how you get when—"

"From me," he interrupted. "You've heard about it from me. I'm self-aware, Bethany, and I'm under control."

"Not just from you."

Now he really appeared wounded.

"What did Chase say?"

"The truth, I would imagine. Have you ever known him not to?"

Trevor paced for a few seconds but didn't argue.

"Chase told me the buzz can be a prologue to the blur-outs. The blur-outs can be a precursor to the hallucinations. You're finally rid of the hallucinations. Do you really want to bring them back?"

He shook his head, but it took a beat too long.

"What?" I said.

Trevor's eyes met mine, and my heart sank.

"Goddamn it, what? Did you blur-out already? We don't even have enough facts for you to come up with any kind of reasonable scenarios, real or imagined."

"No, I didn't blur-out," he said.

"Then, what?"

"We may have had a visitor outside the house this morning."

I waited.

"I think someone was creeping around the back door."

"Okay," I said. "And you think it might be our old friends from the EEDC finally scouting things out?"

"Maybe," he said uncertainly.

"Or?" I prompted.

"Or it was a mailman," he said with no more certainty.

"Or?"

He hesitated. "Or it was a hallucination."

I put a hand up to my face. My head began to ache. "Jesus Christ."

"It was probably a mailman, but I'm not sure why he would have cut through the backyard."

We stared at each other for a long moment.

"None of the killings were in his district."

"What?" I said.

"Why is Sebastian Waterford taking point on this effort? Look at the locations where the bodies were found. He's had no murders in his district, and there is nothing in his background indicating he's looking to make a name for himself so he can make a run at a higher office. In fact, it's almost as if he avoids the spotlight as much as any politician can. So, why insert himself into this case? Why not let the more experienced bureaucrats run the show? Why go behind the scenes and bring us in?"

"I covered this with him this morning."

"You did?"

"Yes. I am pretty good at this, you know."

He nodded. "Of course you are. You're right. What did he say?"

My eyes scanned the wall and once again fell to the desk—the gun. I studied Trevor in his disheveled state. My thoughts drifted back to Chase's wedding and my stupid push for a proposal followed by all the accompanying negative thoughts I'd ignored for too long. Then I did something I hadn't done since I'd fallen in love with Trevor. I walked away.

Chapter 9

Bethany Nolan

"Stay here," Waterford told me. "If you have a notepad, get it out and try to look like a journalist."

Awesome. The last time I'd posed as a journalist, Trevor had blown up a large portion of a city. At least this time I was alone. My conversation with Trevor in his office had concluded with me being embarrassed that I suddenly didn't know how to handle Trevor and him being unsure about his own reality. As for my own reality, I was having to come to terms with the fact that I'd never had to see this side of him. When fate had brought us together, other people—evil people—were trying to pull Trevor's strings and had helped shape his circumstances. Now I was seeing the Trevor Galloway who didn't know where he fit in and seemed to need a puzzle to solve. From what I'd read after first meeting him, and later heard from Chase, if he didn't get his occasional fix from an investigation, he'd get it from a needle or pill. One might think the easy solution would be to let him work cases but, by his own admission, those had proven to be as hazardous to him as any narcotic.

I scribbled nonsense in a notepad and took a few photos of the neighborhood with my phone. It was a nice neighborhood off of Pooler Parkway at the western edge of the county. Waterford had called me at 9:30 PM, and I sped to the scene. With every news outlet having someone perched over a police scanner at 9:11 PM, the suburban cookie-cutter development was crawling with reporters by the time I'd arrived. I stood behind a set of barriers the police had set up near the entrance to the street and listened to chatter between a few of the journalists.

"Not much different than the others."
"Definitely the same guy."
"I heard it was one victim. White female."
"Guess he's branching out—geographically speaking. We're barely in the county way out here."
"Ballsy move, doing it here. I was listening to the scanner and only three minutes and fifteen seconds passed between the call and when the first officer marked on scene."
"So?"
"So. Look at the length of the street. Unless Google Maps is lying to me, it dead-ends right past the crime scene. Hell, look at this neighborhood. There are only two ways in and out of this place. Either the killer called it in after the deed was done and he was already gone, or he's begging to get caught."

More police cars made their way past the barriers and headed toward the scene while a Chatham Emergency Services vehicle exited. Something I'd noticed since moving to the county was that the fire and ambulance services seemed to fall under the umbrella of CES, which was staffed largely by volunteers. Presumably, the victim at the scene was dead, so CES was cut loose.

I watched the taillights of the CES vehicle fade into the distance and realized the reporter I'd overheard was right. The road I'd driven into the housing development was long, and while I'd seen plenty of small side streets terminating in cul-de-sacs, I hadn't seen more than one street that could have led to another way out of the neighborhood. Three minutes and fifteen seconds was not a long time. Assuming the killer did actually make the call at the time of the murder, then how was he not caught or at least spotted?

You're a killer.

You have one hundred ninety-five seconds between you and a potential death sentence.

You're in a decently lit neighborhood lined with narrow streets, and you have limited exit points.

Are you that much of a gambler? Are you crazy? Leaving fast will only draw attent—

Then it hit me.

I held my phone up and started taking photos of everyone around me. Every reporter, every camera operator, and every onlooker. The guy who appeared to have been out walking his dog but was now gawking at the mob of people being corralled along the street—photographed. The lady standing on her porch in a bathrobe—photographed. The guy with the tattoo sleeves, coiling cables into the back of the news truck—photographed.

After a few moments, my actions were noticed. I saw one woman I assumed was a reporter nudge a man with her elbow and mouth something. They both glanced in my direction. A guy with a handlebar mustache turned away when my phone had found his face. There was someone wearing a hoodie, standing right up against one of the barricades, and I started moving around to try to get an angle. I stumbled, nearly falling, and must have made a noise because the figure turned its head slightly in my direction. Suddenly, the person spun away and started walking in the opposite direction. I weaved between several people, bumping into a few, and started to lose ground. The figure began walking rapidly away from the barricade, down the sidewalk, and then shot down a darker side street. Finally, I made it to the corner and stopped behind a large oak. Peering around, I tried to see if the person had scurried up to one of the houses or perhaps run down the street to the cul-de-sac simply in the hopes of my losing interest. I squinted down the street and tried to focus my eyes.

A hand fell onto my shoulder and I spun, propelling my left fist toward where I assumed my attacker's center mass would be. Throwing a punch blind is never ideal, but if you have to—aim for the center of the body rather than the head. The punch was fast. It should have broken a rib or gone straight into my assailant's diaphragm. To my absolute astonishment, my punch never connected with a body and was instead cradled in a large hand.

"I thought you were the calm one," said Sebastian Waterford quietly.

I inhaled deeply.

"Who are we chasing?"

I took another glance down the street.

"Nobody," I said.

"Look. I can't get you in the house, but here's what we're facing."

He pulled out his phone and opened a photo.

"I was able to sneak a couple of pics when nobody was looking my way," he said.

"I'm surprised they let you in at all."

He shrugged. "They're scared now. A city detective might have told me to hit the bricks, but nobody wants to piss off a county commissioner with all the national attention that is going to head our way. The county PD will need the politicians to run interference, or more importantly, to *not* throw any of their people under the bus should these killings continue."

Waterford handed me his phone, and I focused on the photo. Slightly off-center in what appeared to be a living room was the body of an adult female. The woman, wearing a pair of red athletic shorts and a white tank top, was splayed out in the center of a carpeted floor, her lifeless eyes open toward the ceiling.

I scrolled once and another photo appeared on the screen. This shot had been taken from a closer distance and a different angle. From this perspective, I could see a yoga mat laid out a few feet from the body and a water bottle positioned nearby.

Zooming in on the body, I couldn't see any blood or obvious signs of trauma. However, now I noticed the area of carpet around the body was discolored.

"Was she working out?" I asked. "The carpet looks wet, but all that can't be from sweat."

Waterford put his hands in his pockets and scanned the neighborhood as he said, "It's not sweat. It's mostly water from the bathtub."

"The tub?" I thought for a moment and then asked, "Did he drown her in the tub? Who moved the body?"

Waterford nodded. "We won't know for sure until the M.E. examines the body, but it does appear she was drowned in the bathroom. There's water all over the place in that room, so she must have fought hard. Then, he moved her back to the living room."

"Jesus. Who is she?"

Her name is Liza Bak. She is…was supposed to marry one of our dispatchers, Jackson Parker next month. He was on duty tonight but didn't take the 9-1-1 call."

"You said *most* of the moisture on the carpet was water."

"She urinated herself at some point during the attack. We don't know where the attack started, so that could account for some of the discoloration."

"Forced entry?"

"Nothing obvious. No broken glass or kicked-in doors. The front door was locked when officers arrived, but the back door was wide open."

"When can I hear the recording of the 9-1-1 call?"

"I can get it to you tomorrow. I'll get you all the reports and forensic results as they come in as well, but that will take some time."

Another news van pulled down the street. Lights from the headlights passed over us as the driver performed a U-turn to claim an open piece of curb on the other side of the road.

"I assume the cops are checking all the footage from the

traffic cameras near the crime scenes and looking for any vehicles that appear at multiple locations?"

Waterford nodded.

"Did this lady have an alarm system?"

"I'm not sure."

"Did any of the victims?"

"I'd have to go back and check, but I'm sure one or two did. Certainly, the bookstore would have had an alarm system."

"But no alarm activations, right?"

"Right. But how many people set their alarm when they are home and awake? All of the victims have been awake at the time of the attack."

"I suppose," I said.

"What are you thinking?"

"Doesn't it seem weird how sometimes he has to force his way in, but other times he doesn't?"

"I guess he assesses each situation independently. If a door is unlocked, then he'll take advantage of the opportunity. If not, then he finds a way to break in."

"So, we're dealing with a meticulous planner who researches his victims, figures out a point of attack, makes sure to make the call at exactly 9:11 in the evening, kills the person, and escapes without a trace. But when it comes to planning the method of entry, he leaves it to chance? Does that seem right to you?"

"It does seem inconsistent. But I don't think we're dealing with someone completely stable here," said Waterford. Then, looking back toward the house of Liza Bak, he added, "I'm not sure you can pin down the mental state of someone capable of murdering multiple people."

I assumed that last remark wasn't meant to feel personal, yet it did.

Chapter 10

Bethany Nolan

After talking to Waterford, I'd sat in my car and written down detailed notes. It was a habit of mine to rewrite my initial notes, adding as many details as I could remember. Trevor told me my notes were often *too* detailed, but something about having an accurate written account made me feel better. Eventually, I left the scene around 11:00 PM and took a drive around the area since I needed time to think. Also, to be honest, I didn't want to go home. My trip had taken even longer than I'd planned after a pair of headlights had appeared, and remained, in my rearview for several miles once I'd left Waterford. I thought the same car might have reappeared behind me once I got closer to home, but then it turned off. Of course, the last thing I was going to do was tell Trevor about it since he had recently been on the brink of mania paired with paranoia.

    I didn't arrive home until nearly 1:00 AM, and Trevor was still awake. I found him sitting in the living room with a tall drink in his hand. He rarely drank heavily but, given his earlier condition, the thought crossed my mind that he might be drunk. However, as I approached, I saw it appeared he was sipping on nothing more than iced tea. Music was coming from the record player in the corner. A one-of-a-kind album he had acquired during a case was spinning around at a low volume. Our eyes met when I entered the room.

"You didn't need to wait up."

"I couldn't sleep," he said.

I took a seat on the couch opposite him and said, "How are you feeling?"

His stoicism was unreadable, which had been the norm when we had met. Some of his icy demeanor had melted away with me over time, but it was never completely gone. I understood. How could a person who can't trust himself or the intentions of his mind ever truly smile? From what part of the soul would that smile originate? Would it be an expression of joy or one of malice?

Trevor shook his head. "I should be asking you that question."

I shrugged and said, "I couldn't enter the crime scene. I just saw photos."

He turned his head and stared off. "That's not what I meant."

I wasn't sure what to say. It's not as if I hadn't known he came with baggage. Hell, I had practically embraced his past. With my aspirations of becoming a great novelist, simply being around him was a research gold mine. Then, there was the fact I was hopelessly in love with the psychopath. Yeah...that.

"I'll be okay. We've been through a lot, so I'm not sure why seeing you like that bothered me the way it did."

He looked back at me. "Yes, you do."

I didn't speak. In the background, the music played.

"She kept journals," he said finally.

"Who?"

"My mother. I never showed them to you, but they're in a box we have up in the attic. There are probably two dozen of them. Most people would call them diaries, but she called them journals. You can read them if you want."

"Why...why would I—"

"I don't think she was crazy," said Trevor. "I was sitting here thinking about what must always be in the back of your mind when you're dealing with me. Seeing me in that state...a map on the wall, and me ranting, it had to...anyway...now I realize that's what you were getting at when you suggested there could be another cause, other than PTSD, for my hallucinations. That's why you grew concerned when I mentioned my mother listened to music on headphones, even when she was alone. You thought she might be trying to drown out voices in her head or ignore her own hallucinations. It's been a long time since I looked at the journals, but I think you'll see there is nothing in the writing to indicate mental illness."

"So, you've read all of her private journals?" I asked, surprised.

"Of course."

"When? Why?"

"Years ago. And I did so because I shot and killed Lukas Derela in a motel room. Then, the prick kept showing up in my life. I work puzzles—that's what I do. So, of course, I worked every angle regarding the origins of my hallucinations. I went down the same path you find yourself going now. The only question I have for you is: Why now? You've known about my problems. None of this is new information to you. I've done some horrible things, and I even tried to warn you off several times. Was it Chase's wedding? Because if you don't want to get married, then I understand. We can keep things the way they are. That is, if you're willing to stay with me."

"It's not marriage that scares me," I said.

"Then...what?"

I hesitated. "A kid."

His stony demeanor started to break apart and he leaned forward in his chair. "Are you...?"

My hands shot up as I realized my mistake. "I'm not. I'm not pregnant. However, I think I want to be someday."

Trevor leaned back and, for the life of me, I couldn't tell if he was relieved or disappointed. *Damn you, Tin Man.*

"You're afraid my condition is hereditary," he said.

I nodded.

"Is that all?"

I shook my head.

"What else? The EEDC? Because we can relocate if you want. We can change our names. The odds are they'll never find us this time."

"It's not just that," I said.

"Then, what?"

I waited a beat. "At your age, I don't want you to hurt yourself in bed."

His head fell. Eventually, he looked up, and I tried not to smile but failed miserably in that department as some of the tension left the room.

Trevor took a long drink of his tea and said, "Tell me about the crime scene."

I yawned. "Tomorrow. Waterford should have the actual 9-1-1 recording and the preliminary reports to me tomorrow anyway. I wrote up detailed notes for you to look over if you want."

"Where are they?"

I stood. "Tomorrow," I said again. I reached out my hand, he took it, and I pulled him to his feet. "In the meantime, come upstairs with me. I might have just enough energy to see how injury-prone you are."

Trevor's face relaxed. He might not trust himself, but he did trust me. I would have to do my best to return the favor no matter what.

Chapter 11

Trevor Galloway

"I'll still need to see some identification."

Bethany stepped forward. For the second time, she said, "Mr. Waterford is expecting us. Please let him know we are here."

We had already tried to call and text Sebastian Waterford but hadn't gotten a reply. The heavyset woman behind the glass made no effort to hide her annoyance. She was in her early thirties and had probably been pretty before life did its thing.

"Nobody enters the communications center without a pass. To issue you a pass, I need to verify you have been approved and then log your identification into the system. No ID, no pass."

Through gritted teeth, Bethany said, "Tell him his guests are here."

Under normal circumstances, we would have been fine handing over our identifications, but Waterford still wanted our involvement in the case to be kept quiet. Therefore, he had told us to arrive at the front desk and tell the receptionist we were there for a meeting with him. Now it seemed we were potentially entangled in a bureaucratic whirlpool not uncommon with any local government.

"I can't call his extension because he doesn't have an office here," she said. "And it wouldn't be right for me to page him over the loudspeakers since I don't know who you are and if he's really expecting you. I can't leave the desk and go searching the whole building for him. Look, I'm not losing my job because some person off the street wants to talk to a county commissioner."

Bethany threw her arms up and turned away from the woman, who I could now see had her name on a sign behind the glass. I moved forward and could see Crystal Stewart kept an orderly desk. To her right were the phone, a notepad, and a calendar book turned to this week. A bank of monitors was arranged behind the phone, displaying images of several building entrances and a few angles of the parking lot. In one monitor, I saw what appeared to be the Lexus that Waterford had driven to our office the day we had met.

To Crystal's left were family photos. There were pictures of her with a plump little girl who had to have been her daughter and a few with a bearded man who seemed to have no resemblance to the little girl. Crystal and the man were kissing in one photo, and another photo was of him alone in firefighter gear. She wasn't wearing a wedding band, so I made the assumption he was a boyfriend. Directly in front of her was a printed-out spreadsheet that she began writing on as I approached the glass. It was when she moved her right arm to scribble something on the sheet that I noticed something else. For a split second, the short sleeve of her blouse had raised above her bicep, revealing four distinct bruises. The marks were finger-sized, as if someone had grabbed her arm hard. However we were going to get cooperation, force wasn't the way. She was probably getting enough of that at home, and work was the one place *she* had the control.

"You're an impossible spot," I said.

She didn't glance up from the paper in front of her.

"Sorry. It must seem like we're putting you in a no-win situation," I said.

Now she looked up.

"You can't go searching for Mr. Waterford and, for all you

know, we're a couple of nuts who want to bitch at him about our neighborhood trash collection. Of course you can't page him. He'd be furious if it turned out he got ambushed by crazy constituents with a cause."

Crystal nodded, ever so slightly, and her expression started to soften. I began to turn away, and she started to look down again. Then I turned back and said, "However, this is an important meeting, and he's going to be *furious* if you don't tell him we're here." Now, worry began to register on her face. This possibility hadn't occurred to her. I said, "We don't want you to get in trouble either way, so maybe we can come up with a solution."

Crystal turned her head from side to side, as if a solution might be coming around the corner. When one didn't, her eyes returned to me.

"I know what Mr. Waterford's car looks like," I said.

"So?"

"So, if suspicious characters like the two of us…" I waved a hand between Bethany and myself. "If we were outside hanging around Mr. Waterford's car, wouldn't you be obligated to let him know? I mean…that would be a safety issue. It would be reckless *not* to say anything. He would probably check the monitors connected to the security cameras I saw outside and be able to see who we are. If he doesn't know us, he'll have the cops come talk to us. If he does, then he'll invite us in, and we won't tell him about us having this conversation with you. In the end, you will have done your duty and you won't be running the risk of being responsible for Mr. Waterford having personal contact with a couple of crazies, because he'll have a chance to see us first."

Crystal Stewart's eyes shifted, rose, then brightened. It seemed she was about to say something, but then simply nodded. I pivoted and saw Bethany was already headed toward the exit. I followed, happy our client had asked for my presence and that my partner hadn't objected. While some of the smoke had cleared between the two of us and I wished Bethany had wanted me to come along so I could lend my insights, I suspected the truth was she figured she would worry less about me if I were by her side than if I were home alone with my ill-behaved mind.

"Okay," Bethany said as we arrived at the Lexus. "That was smooth."

I leaned against the car, crossed my arms, and said, "I'm legendary for my charisma."

She sighed and rolled her eyes. Her reaction felt good. It felt...normal.

"How did you know that was the way to play her?"

"The receptionist? I noticed—"

My explanation was interrupted by the sound of a crash bar opening a door on the side of the building. Sebastian Waterford peered out and then waved for us to head in his direction.

He held the door open and said, "The receptionist told me a couple of people were hanging around my car. Why didn't you just go to the lobby?"

Bethany and I shot each other a quick glance.

She said, "We figured they might want some I.D. or something, and you do want to keep our involvement reasonably quiet. I did try to call and text you."

Waterford reached into his suit jacket and retrieved his phone. "Dammit. I left it on silent and didn't feel it vibrate. Sorry about that."

He led us down a long, nondescript corridor. The building looked and smelled institutional. The lighting was institutional. Our footsteps sounded institutional. Low government bid construction did wonders for creating a hospitable atmosphere. We made a right at the end of the hallway and button-hooked again into a small conference room. On one side of the lone table sat a white mustached man in his fifties and an Asian-American woman who wouldn't hit her fifties for at least half a decade. Positioned at one end of the table was a shaggy-haired man who appeared as if he might have left a Jimmy Buffett concert. He barely glanced up from his phone as we entered, while the other two at the table stood.

Not waiting to be introduced, the woman said, "I'm Jill Koll. I've just learned of your involvement in this case and I'm still weighing the implications. Obviously, your inclusion could create all sorts of legal issues and," she shot a look toward Waterford, "should word get out you were brought in, the morale of the unit could be negatively affected."

Koll dressed professionally and wore her hair in a tight bun. Her approach bore the scuff marks of a detective, but her vocabulary had the polish of an attorney. I immediately liked her, although I doubted the feeling was mutual.

"Jill is the senior investigator from the Chatham County side of the house," Waterford explained, obviously uncomfortable with Koll's directness and lack of respect for protocol. "And this is Wayne Downey. He's the lead detective for Savannah PD."

Downey came around the table and shook our hands. He was wearing khakis and a tucked-in polo shirt that accentuated the fact that he was carrying an extra thirty pounds above a belt on which a Savannah PD badge was clipped near a holstered gun.

"Welcome to the clusterfuck," he said from underneath a horseshoe mustache before heading back around the table and retaking his seat.

Without enthusiasm, Waterford gestured to the shaggy-haired man whose attention was still on the phone in his hands. "This is Dean Hudson. He's the 9-1-1 center director."

Hudson didn't make any pretense of having the slightest thought of getting out of his chair or shaking our hands. However, the man, wearing a well-used T-shirt sporting the name of a local pizza chain, did offer up a curt nod before taking his attention back to the phone in his lap.

Bethany and I introduced ourselves in a general sense, not knowing what our role was supposed to be, and then we all took seats around the table. All eyes fell on Waterford, who had dark circles under his eyes. I noticed his unbreachable sense of competence was missing. Obviously, something had changed since he had decided to bring us into the fold, but there was something different about him on a personal level. I couldn't be certain, but he seemed to be exuding an emotion I knew all too well.

"Detectives Koll and Downey are leading the task force assigned to the 9-1-1 killings," Waterford explained. "Director Hudson had the misfortune of taking over the communication center a few weeks before the killings started." Waving a hand around the table, Waterford said, "I've explained to everyone here how I brought in outside consultants and how they are not to disseminate this information to anyone. It had been my hope that Ms. Nolan and Mr. Galloway would be able to work independently—in a vacuum—but another person has been killed and, according to Detectives Koll and Downey, we are no closer to discovering the identity of the killer. Therefore, I've decided it's time to collaborate to the greatest extent possible without undermining the morale of the task force or creating potential legal complications should this suspect be brought to trial."

"Also because you were spotted at the most recent crime scene talking to Ms. Nolan, which prompted questions from the chief of police," said Jill Koll.

Waterford stared her down and a definite chill passed through the room.

With steel in his eyes, Waterford said, "There was some confusion as to whom I might have been speaking since there were several reporters at the scene. Someone had mistakenly thought Ms. Nolan might have been working for one of the local media outlets, so I made it clear to your chief that I was not speaking to any journalists and, yes, that did lead me to explain Ms. Nolan's involvement. It was decided a quiet but collaborative approach would be explored."

It didn't take much to read between the lines. Waterford had been caught between a rock and a hard place. Koll's chief had told Waterford that his private investigation into the murders would become semi-private, or it was about to become extremely public.

Downey, in some attempt to break the tension, smiled and leaned forward on the table. He looked at Bethany and me. "Look, I'm glad to meet you two. I really am. And I don't mean any offense here and I'm not one for territorial pissing matches, but I'm not exactly clear on what a couple of P.I.s bring to the table. We have plenty of experienced investigators on the task force. Savannah is a hotbed for homicides. Sadly, we work forty or fifty per year in the city limits. It's kind of in our wheelhouse."

"That's a fair concern," I replied.

Koll said, "And I don't want to see us arrest the perp and then watch him walk because a defense attorney gets wind of your involvement. What if you touch a piece of evidence and taint the chain of custody? What if you talk to a witness and end up on the stand? Your credibility can be questioned. I don't know your history. Will the case get tossed out because of something in your past? There are a lot of unknowns here."

"Also reasonable," said Bethany.

Nobody spoke for several long seconds until Hudson, becoming aware this appeared to be the time to air any concerns about our involvement in the case, looked up from his phone and placed it on the table.

"Do you know how many calls we take per year?" he asked, looking at Bethany and me. "Approximately seven hundred thousand. That's eight to ten times more than the surrounding counties."

Now he stood, and we could see he was wearing shorts to go with his T-shirt. He leaned forward and placed his hands on the table.

"Our staffing was struggling to stay at eighty percent of what it should be *before* the family members of my communication officers were murdered. Now we are closer to fifty percent and dropping." He tapped an index finger on the table for emphasis and then looked around the table. "This was my first day off in a month. I finally get a day to take the boat out—a boat I'd live on if I could—but then I get a call that I need to rush in for a meeting with a county commissioner and parties unknown only to be told that a couple of private investigators have been hired as consultants on the down-low." Hudson raised his eyes to the ceiling and brought his hands up in a surrendering expression. "Bullshit. This is all bullshit."

Waterford tried to interject. "Dean, this has been frustrat—"

To my surprise, Hudson jabbed a finger in Waterford's direction and became more irritated. If a county commissioner held any power over Hudson's job, he certainly didn't seem to care.

"I've already wasted enough time on this." He then spun toward Koll and Downey. "Do you hear me? No more wasting my time looking for needles in haystacks. Instead of bothering the few employees I have left, why don't you get out there and find this guy? Don't drag me in here and expect me to get on board with this…" he stared at Bethany and me as if we were mosquitoes in his tent. "This gimmick!"

With that, he stormed out of the room, and a moment of quiet descended upon the group.

"Okie dokie. Glad we all understand each other," said Downey with a grin, breaking the silence.

Waterford sat up straighter and directed his words toward the task force detectives. "I realize this is unorthodox, and I get your concerns. However, there's more upside than downside in working with Ms. Nolan and Mr. Galloway. I still want word of their involvement to remain within our small group. Even if they find a vital clue that ultimately breaks the case, I don't want it known that I've contracted outside assistance. It's unconventional at best, and—let me be honest here—it makes it appear that I don't have faith in our local police resources. Which I assure you is not the case."

"Yes, some might say it appears that way," said Koll in a tone that made it clear she was one of the *some*.

Waterford started to speak again, but I interrupted.

"What's the priority, detectives?" I asked.

The detectives didn't reply.

"Right now. This second. What is the priority? It's not a trick question."

"Stop the killer before he kills again," said Koll.

"Okay. We all agree on that. Let's start there. Everything else is secondary. Right now, we aren't doing anything but reviewing paperwork, photos, and recordings. However, it would be helpful if we had more access and could talk to some people. Of course, we don't want to jeopardize any future prosecution. We'll play by the rules and keep you informed of our actions. But the main thing is we stop this guy before he kills again."

The detectives seemed to mull this over. I thought I'd made a compelling case. I was wrong.

Koll swiveled toward Waterford. "I can't go along with this. Unless my chief orders me to give them access, then it's not happening. With all due respect, Chief Fenton gets a lot of calls from the county commissioners, and you're just one. I doubt he'll cave on this demand."

Waterford looked at Downey who shrugged a shoulder and said, "I'm all for more brainpower, but I have to agree with Jill on this one. We may have too many chefs in the kitchen as it is, and I don't see how this helps matters."

Waterford sighed. "You have no solid leads. Why not go outside the box on this one?"

"Why should we trust these two? How do we know they are competent in the least?" asked Koll.

Waterford had no counterargument. We had worked on the case for a short time only and received information piecemeal. In addition to that, Bethany and I hadn't truly been functioning as a team and she'd been keeping me in the background for good reason. Perhaps the detectives were right after all and our involvement was counterproductive at best. I was starting to resign myself to walking away from the case when Bethany spoke up.

"Give Trevor all the reports, crime scene photos, recordings, and thirty minutes to go over them."

"What?" several of us said in unison.

She repeated the request and added, "You've been working the case for weeks. If Trevor doesn't come up with something you didn't have after thirty minutes of reviewing the materials, then we walk away. However, if he comes up with something tangible—something that is relevant to the killer's M.O. or identity, then we get full access moving forward, no further debates."

Koll began, "I don't see how—"

"Twenty minutes," Bethany countered.

"Oh, hell. Why not?" said Downey, smiling. "I like roulette. Let's spin the wheel. Do you want hard copies, or are the electronic files okay?"

"Electronic are fine, but it helps if we can set up dual monitors. Three monitors if possible."

Downey stood. "I've got my laptop in the car and can get access to the network. We'll set it up in here. Maybe Mr. Waterford and Jill can scrounge up some monitors and whatever cords we need to hook them up."

The others in the group started shuffling out of the conference room, and I turned toward Bethany. "What on Earth are you doing?"

"We were about to get shut down."

"That may have been for the best."

"Would it?"

"What do you mean?"

"I mean, you need a puzzle and you're going to seek one out one way or another. I don't want to come home to find you spiraling into insanity."

"If you're asking me to do in a few minutes what I think you're asking me to do, then I'm a little confused as to where we stand. It's possible this may not be good for me—for us."

"I'm saying I'm with you for the entire ride. We're going to do this as a team, and we can't do it with one arm tied behind our back. Keeping you holed up in a room with a computer isn't going to work on this case. I don't want either of us to feel responsible for someone else getting killed on account of us being afraid of letting you do what you're good at. So, do your thing and we'll deal with the consequences, whatever they may be."

"Are you sure about this?"

"No."

"Good. Because I may not find anything."

She put a hand on my face. "Yes, you will. There is something wrong and inconsistent with the way the killer enters the homes. There is something wrong with all of this. I'm not seeing it, but you will if you let yourself."

"What then? What if the other things come back?"

"We've lived with them before," she said. "The house is too big for two people anyway."

Chapter 12

Trevor Galloway

"You can use the laptop screen as a third monitor if you need to," Downey explained as he finished walking me through the organization of the electronic files. We were alone in the conference room; everyone else had vacated to whatever offices were available. "It was lucky I was able to snag you a regular mouse, so you don't have to use the trackpad on the laptop. Remember not to exit out of the network or let it time out, or I'll have to log you back in with my password. Some of the scanned-in handwritten notes are hard to decipher, and the report formats vary depending on where the murder occurred." Downey paused and then said, "You know, Waterford didn't give me your background. Are you familiar with law enforcement terminology? Are you going to be able to make sense of the reports? I mean, you act like a cop, but I thought I better ask."

"I was a cop," I said without further explanation.

"All right. Well, let me know if you have any questions with the local terminology. I'll be next door. Honestly, I don't care how long you take, but I have a feeling Koll is starting the clock on you as soon as I close that door. If I were you, I'd expect to see her in twenty minutes flat. Good luck."

He started to leave, but I stopped him. "Hey, what did Hudson mean with all that talk about not wasting any more time and looking for needles in haystacks?"

Downey turned back around. "We've had his administrative staff data mining, so to speak."

"You've had them looking for possible leaks and trying to figure out who has access to information about the families of the dispatchers," I said. "You know the killer has to be getting information from the inside."

Downey's mustache twitched. "It's highly likely, but not necessarily the case. We live in the information age, and nearly anything you want to know is available if you know how to search for it online. Tracking down relatives, even distant relatives of dispatchers, isn't a heavy lift for someone with an understanding of search tools and public records."

"I would think Hudson would be extremely motivated to assist you and would be fairly receptive to accepting help from anyone and everyone. I mean, these are the family members of his employees being killed."

Downey's mustache drooped on both sides. "I've said the same thing. But I know he's under unimaginable stress. It's hard to guess how a man will react when the bodies start dropping."

He turned away, shut the door, and I went to work. Having already used a wall in my home to map out the districts in which the killer had struck, I made a mental note of the most recent murder and put geography aside for the moment. I dedicated one monitor to incident reports. The second monitor was displaying the related field notes, forensic reports, and statements from neighbors. The third was reserved for photographs and sketches of the crime scenes. I'd heard most of the 9-1-1 calls but had not listened to the one from the Liza Bak killing. I opened a folder containing that audio file and prompted it to play.

Chatham 9-1-1.
Tick.
Hello? Chatham 9-1-1. What is your emergency?

Tock.
What is…oh no…please, God. What is your…
Tick. Tock. Tick. Tock. Tick. Tock.
59 Tranquil Place, Pooler.

The call ended. Something occurred to me, and I pulled up the initial incident report for the Liza Bak homicide. I scrolled through the narrative, finding what I was looking for. Then I pulled up the reports of the other killings and compared the information. Quickly, I pulled up the recordings of the 9-1-1 calls and confirmed what had been noted in the reports. The killer had given the dispatchers the address in some, but not all of the calls. It depended on how he made the call. If the victim had a landline, he would use it to make the call, suspecting the address would register with the Chatham County Dispatch Center. If the victim didn't have a landline, then the killer used the victim's cell phone to place the call and gave dispatchers the address. Either the killer didn't have any qualms about making quick decisions under pressure, or he already knew whether the victims had landlines.

I took a few minutes to skim through the incident reports, although I'd read most of them previously. What I hadn't seen were many photographs and sketches. Most of the images were focused on the bodies and the areas surrounding the bodies, but Bethany had told me something was bugging her about the points of entry. Fortunately, each file contained photographs of the doors or windows where the killer had made his way into the home or business. I spent several minutes scrutinizing the details of those photographs. The scenes showed no signs of forced entry at all, which muddied the waters further.

I pulled up the photographs from the first crime scene where Ted Whittle had been burned alive in his garage. A glass pane next to a side door had been broken, and the killer had simply reached in and opened the door from the inside. Then he proceeded to sneak up on Whittle and strike him in the head before tying him up and setting him ablaze. A street-view photo of the front of the house was included in the folder as well.

Marleen Daughtry was strangled to death four weeks later in her own home. The killer had somehow gotten in the back door or been let in the house, put his hands around her throat, and squeezed. Investigators had taken scores of photos of the interior and exterior of the home, understanding this murder was connected to the Whittle scene. There were photos of the street, the neighbors' homes, the cars on the street…everything.

Taylor LaFreniere had her throat slit and hands cut off while doing inventory in a downtown Savannah bookstore. Although the store was supposed to be closed, investigators found no sign of forced entry. LaFreniere's husband said she never would have left the door to the store unlocked while she was doing inventory.

Next, Elena Zacaba and Rodrigo and Juan Ortiz were gunned down in an apartment while communications officer Alicia Montez sat helplessly in the dispatch center. There were no signs of forced entry, and the use of a loud firearm in an apartment complex suggested a growing boldness on the part of the killer.

Finally, I pulled up the photos from the recent killing. Liza Bak had been attacked, presumably drowned in a bathtub and then placed in the middle of the living room floor. Again, no signs of forced entry were evident and, in this instance, the killer not only dared the police to catch him but nearly cornered himself on a dead-end street—if he left at all. If he was in uniform, then he may have blended into the scene as first responders arrived. Police had found the front door locked but the back door open upon arriving, so perhaps Liza had been careless. I scrolled through the crime scene photos, noting the position of the body and the discolored carpeting. As was the case with the photos of the other scenes, the exterior shots gave me nearly three-hundred-sixty-degree views of the locations.

Multiple methods of entry.
Multiple methods of communication with the police.

Multiple methods of murder.
Zero forensic clues.

I dropped my eyes from the screens arranged around me. The room around me began to fade to black before snippets of the pages of reports and notes flooded into my mind. The sentences and broken paragraphs moved to the sides, and scenes produced from the crime scene photographs materialized in the room before it transformed into Ted Whittle's garage. I stood against a wall and watched as he struggled against his restraints, bound to a chair. Looking around the area, I saw tools arranged on a pegboard, a lawn mower, a weed whacker, a hedge clipper, and an assortment of gardening supplies. Suddenly, without warning, he burst into flames and began screaming. The garage filled with smoke, and I retreated out the door the killer had opened by reaching in through a broken glass panel. While keeping my eyes on the house, I moved toward the front until I got to the front door.

The scene morphed into Marleen Daughtry's house, and I found myself staring at her front porch. I took a moment to note any similarities or differences and then moved around to the back door that had been used by the killer. Once inside, I saw Marleen standing at the kitchen sink. In an instant, her back arched and her hands jolted upward in an effort to defend herself from an attacker I couldn't see. In less than two brutal minutes, she was on the floor, dead.

The cabinets in the Daughtry kitchen became incoherent waves and eventually mutated into bookshelves. I stood inches from the mutilated body of Taylor LaFreniere. Moments earlier, she would have been doing routine inventory in her bookstore, and now her hands were missing. For what purpose? It was highly unlikely a business owner in downtown Savannah would leave a door unlocked in the late evening while alone and running to and from the back of the store. So, why no forced entry? I walked to the front of the store and examined the front door, which was unremarkable. I looked around the street. *Too bad there were no cameras*, I thought. *Wait! That's*—

Something I thought I'd noticed struck me, and I tried to will myself to go back to one of the other scenes, but suddenly I was standing next to Liza Bak who was being pushed underwater in her tub. She was still in her workout clothes and was presumably preparing a bath when the killer entered the house. Had he come in through an open back door?

I walked away from her drowning to see the open door. As noted in the report and seen in the photos, it was unlocked and there were no signs it had been tampered with. I walked outside and went to the front of the house. There it was. On the front porch. Then I thought of the other porches, but not always the porches of the victims—the porches of the neighbors across the street. The police had captured images of most of those porches in photographs.

You clever, sick bastard. You're no psychopath. No, sir. You're no psychopath at all.

"Hey, I'm not kidding."

The porch disintegrated and the monitors took form. My environment went from suburban and HOA compliant to institutional in a matter of disheartening seconds.

"Your time is up," said Jill Koll, leading everyone else into the room.

I rubbed my eyes and nodded while everyone took their original seats. Bethany moved close beside me and patted my arm.

"You okay?"

I told her I was. I didn't know if that was true, but I needed it to be.

Downey leaned back in his chair and grinned. "Well, how did the old ball fall on the roulette wheel?"

I took a breath and steadied myself. The transition back after blur-outs can sometimes be a little disconcerting. It was hard to know where to begin. They weren't going to want to hear what I had to say, but the truth doesn't give way to sympathy.

"Mr. Galloway?" said Koll. "Are you going to dazzle us and tell us who the killer is?"

"No," I said. "I have no idea."

Koll appeared satisfied. Waterford looked depressed. Downey seemed more entertained than anything else.

"But I can tell you *what* he is," I said. "If you'll let me tell you the *what*, and my reasons for believing this, I think you'll like what I have to say."

Chapter 13

Trevor Galloway

"They did *not* like that," said Bethany as she weaved between cars on the interstate.

My head ached. I leaned back, closed my eyes, and fruitlessly tried to slow down my brain. Thoughts and images still raced through my head, but now as flat snapshots rather than immersive scenes. My pulse was too fast. The *high* feeling I needed to control was surging through me like gasoline in my veins. Even the cool reaction I'd received from Downey and Koll hadn't been enough to temper the buzz.

Bethany hit the steering wheel. "Damn it!"

I kept my eyes closed, but they were still seeing. "It's my fault. I should have sold it better."

Analytic bluntness was always a weakness of mine. The only time I could turn on the charm was when I needed to get a confession out of a suspect. Then, I was all about building rapport and verbally painting a picture for the suspect. The picture would be one of near murky hopelessness except for that one beacon of light in the darkness. I held that light. If the suspect would cooperate, simply confess to the crime, then I—who *always* had a brother, sister, or close cousin who had been in the *exact* same situation—would go to bat for the suspect with the D.A. I would pull strings for this particular suspect because I empathized with his situation. Of course, it was all theater on my part, but in those situations, I could play whatever role was needed and smooth-talk the most reluctant of audiences. Not on this day. One of the mysteries of life is that it can be easier to sell jail time to criminals than it is to peddle hard truths to cops.

I opened my eyes, sensing Bethany was slowing the car. We had hit a construction zone, lost a lane of traffic, and now had to crawl along with a centipede of others trying to head east.

Bethany said, "Everything you said made sense."

I didn't respond. Everyone in the room knew my conclusions made sense, but many things make sense. Amputations make sense in a lot of cases, but nobody wants to sacrifice a limb.

"The varying points of entry," she continued. "They should have seen it, but they didn't. How could they have missed it?"

"Too many eyes. Too many moving parts," I said.

"The killer avoided doorbell cameras. Ted Whittle and Liza Bak had doorbell cameras, so, of course, the killer had to find other ways inside."

"The police noticed those."

"But you saw that Marleen Daughtry's neighbor across the street had one as well. And since the killer avoided going in her front door, then we aren't dealing with a fool."

We crept along at five miles per hour. I could see a construction crew piddling around ahead on the right shoulder.

"Taylor LaFreniere's bookstore didn't have a doorbell cam and neither did Elena Zacaba's apartment," Bethany said. "So, your theory as to why there was no forced entry fits when you consider the other factors."

"I think so," I said.

"I mean, you're right. All of the killer's taunts seem to have a common thread. 'Time. Rush. Tick-Tock. Run along.' And he's cutting it close—challenging the police to get there on time. He has the ability to locate the family members of dispatchers, and he knows the average response times to different areas."

I nodded. Something ahead had caught my attention, but I wasn't sure why. I'd spotted something out of place among the construction workers who were milling around between two dump trucks.

"So how did the killer, who knows how to track people down and understands response times, manage to get inside houses without kicking in doors?" she asked rhetorically. "Of course they didn't want to hear the answer!"

"In my defense, I didn't say the magic word."

"Right. You said 'first responder,' but you know what they heard."

"Once I said the killer may have not *immediately* left the scene after killing Liza Bak, they jumped to one conclusion."

There it was again. Ahead. As a car moved out of my line of sight. A flash of a denim jacket and long hair. *No, no, no.*

"They heard you say that the killer was a cop. Which makes sense because who doesn't open the door for a cop?"

Our car edged forward even with the dump trucks, and I looked over all the workers on the side of the road. No denim jacket. No long, greasy hair. No neck tattoos—at least none I'd seen before. In short, no dead drug dealers fighting their way back into my world after my blur-out. *Close the door, Trevor. Close the door.*

"Do you?"

"What?" I asked.

"I said, do you think Waterford believes you?"

I took a breath and rubbed a hand through my hair, feeling a scar left from a bullet.

"I think we have bigger questions to answer."

"Such as?"

We broke free of the traffic jam, and I did my best to allow my thoughts to flow free as well. "Let me ask you this. Did Downey or Koll strike you as incompetent?"

"Well, they missed the doorbell camera across the street from Marleen Daughtry."

"True, but they farm out assignments to, and manage other, investigators. Not everyone can be an all-star. But, on the surface, do the two of them seem incapable in any way?"

Bethany thought for a moment. "No."

"And can we agree that Waterford could call in the feds pretty much any time?"

"As high profile as this case is becoming—absolutely. Why? Is something about Waterford still bothering you?"

"Tell me everything about your meeting with him in the coffee shop. I know you gave me some of the case information Waterford relayed to you, but tell me about him personally. Try to remember everything he said to you and everything he did during your interaction with him. I want to know every detail."

Bethany went on to recount her meeting with Waterford, filling in some of the more mundane details she wouldn't have bothered mentioning to me if I had not asked. I didn't stop her until she mentioned him getting up and walking away at one point. She had continued talking, but I stopped her.

"Wait. Go back. He limped?"

"A little. Just for a minute or two."

"What kind of limp? What leg was he favoring?"

"It was just a limp. He straightened out after a few moments. I think he was favoring his right leg. Why?"

"Was it a limp as if his foot fell asleep, or something more serious?"

"I'd say it was more serious, but like I said, he recovered."

"Okay, keep going."

Bethany finished the story as she steered us toward our home.

She said, "You're suspicious as to why he called us in on this case."

"Extremely. Although they've missed some items, I think he has a rather competent investigative team and he could call in the FBI anytime he wanted to. This crap about *thinking outside the box* doesn't sound right to me. He's hiding something."

"What do you want to do?"

"I want to dig."

Bethany pulled the car into our driveway. Out of habit, we both surveyed the area before she turned off the car.

"I need to make a trip to Augusta. I know Waterford said he would talk to Koll and Downey and try to smooth things over and keep us involved, but that may take a couple of days. In the meantime, I want to see if I can find out more about our employer."

"Okay," Bethany said. "While you're doing that, I think I need to take an unofficial look at that 9-1-1 center director, Dean Hudson. Did he seem right to you?"

"Not in the slightest. He's overly defensive, to say the least."

Bethany shut off the car, but neither of us made a move to get out.

"This was nice," she said.

"Working together to get kicked off a case? We've had better days."

She took my hand. "At least we're working to—"

The back windshield shattered an instant before blood covered the dashboard.

Bethany slumped down in the driver's seat as I tried to look behind us. I yelled her name when another shot rang out and a bullet whizzed between our heads. I opened my door, got out, and drew my Sig Sauer P250. I saw a muzzle flash erupt from a red Honda across the street, and another round zipped past me. I returned fire at the sole occupant of the vehicle, who was wearing a black balaclava. My shots hit the driver's side door, and the shooter peeled out and sped off down the road. It was all so loud, violent, and impossibly quick. The entire episode lasted maybe five seconds.

"Bethany!"

I reholstered the gun, rushed over to her door, and pulled it open.

No, no, no. Not again. Not her.

Gently pushing her back against the seat, I said, "Stay with me. Stay with me."

Her eyes were open, looking at me. "Did you get the shooter?"

"Where are you hit?" I asked.

"It's just my shoulder," she replied. "Did you get the shooter?" she asked again.

"No. Whoever it was drove away. I couldn't even get a look at his or her eyes."

She shook her head in mock frustration. "You had one job. One damn job."

I dug my phone out of my pocket and paused. I didn't think this was an attack by the EEDC. The drug gang enforcers didn't do drive-bys. They liked to make their kills personal, which meant this was related to the current case. Additionally, we had just left a meeting in which I'd proposed a controversial and dangerous scenario to a limited circle of people. Forty minutes and one traffic jam later, we'd been shot at. At the very least, it was likely someone in the building notified the shooter we were there and, possibly, when we were leaving. That was, unless the shooter had been *inside* the building the entire time we were there. I realized that by making a simple phone call I might be indirectly updating our adversary because of who I had to call. However, given Bethany's injury, I had no choice. I gazed at my phone and pressed the buttons. I dialed 9-1-1.

Chapter 14

Trevor Galloway

"She'll have protection round the clock."

"From who?" I asked, throwing my hands in the air. An orderly edged his way around me as I took up too much space in the hospital hallway.

Waterford made a calming gesture. "I get along with the Chief of Savannah PD. I'll have him handpick—"

"No chance," I said. "I stated that the facts indicated a cop might be involved in the killings, and someone shot at us a short time later. That's not a coincidence. I'm not leaving Bethany's side and trusting cops I don't know to keep her safe while she's recovering."

Waterford considered this and said, "I understand." He put a hand on my shoulder. I don't like being touched, but I could tell his concern was sincere. "I really do. How long do the doctors think she might be here?"

"Three or four days," I said. "The bullet didn't hit any major organs and passed right through. It was a handgun round. The detectives who showed up here haven't told me the caliber."

"Did you get the license plate of the car?"

I shook my head. "He pulled away at an angle."

Waterford paced back and forth while stroking his chin.

"What?" I asked.

"If you're right, you have to be out there working this. You saw the reaction of the detectives in the room. They don't want this to be a cop."

"I'm not leaving Bethany exposed so I can run around playing P.I."

"What if you knew she was truly protected?"

"I'm not trusting rent-a-cops either, Waterford. I love her."

"No private security. Feds."

I hesitated. "The case isn't federal yet."

"Isn't it? Let's say you saw U.S. Government plates on that car."

"On a red Honda?" I said dryly. I assumed Waterford realized most cars used by the government were Fords, Chevys, and Dodges.

"So, perhaps the government plates were stolen. Either way, Bethany is a witness and a victim of a crime that now has a federal nexus. And I so happen to be on speaking terms with the U.S. Attorney for the Southern District of Georgia. How would you like two Deputy U.S. Marshals to be posted outside Bethany's room while she's recovering?"

"Not as much as if I was in arm's reach."

Waterford nodded and said, "Is she sleeping right now?"

I said she was.

"I don't know her well—so, correct me if I'm wrong—but I get the impression that if she finds out you plan on cozying up beside her for several days while a killer is out there waiting to strike again, she's going to be less than receptive to that idea."

I looked away. "That's correct."

"So, how about you help catch this bastard before he hurts someone else? I'll have her protected within the hour and then you can explain the situation to her when she wakes up."

"I already told the cops I didn't get the tags on the shooter's car."

Waterford shrugged. "You were in shock. It came back to

you. Memory is a funny thing when you're under fire."

"You know from experience?" I asked.

A shadow seemed to fall over his face. "I've been around."

Once Bethany had come to, she had playfully chastised me for missing the shooter when I'd fired. The police arrived after the ambulance, since EMTs had only to respond from the nearby fire station. The cops talked to Bethany while the EMTs attended to her wound, and she backed my story that it was *her* gun I'd grabbed when we had been attacked. I'd already placed the gun on the passenger seat floorboard and stuffed the holster I'd been wearing in the glovebox. The problem was I didn't *technically* have the right to possess a gun in the state of Georgia since I'd been committed to a psychiatric institution in the past, but nobody could fault me for returning fire in this situation. Unfortunately, the police had taken my…or Bethany's gun. Fortunately, we had more at the house.

The original plan had been for Bethany to look into Dean Hudson while I traveled to Augusta to learn a little more about Sebastian Waterford. However, with Bethany out of commission and me not wanting to be more than a few minutes away from the hospital, I decided I would check out the 9-1-1 center director and let Waterford be for the moment.

As promised, deputy marshals arrived at the hospital and took up position outside Bethany's room. Waterford then gave me a ride back to my house. The Volkswagen, still in the driveway with the keys in the ignition, was filled with shattered glass and had been processed for evidence. I walked past it, entered the house, reached up, and turned off the alarm system. It was then I realized my arms still had traces of Bethany's blood on them. *Someone had shot Bethany.* I gnashed my teeth together, brought my hands down, and clenched my fists. Looking down, I saw her blood was on my shirt as well. I began walking toward the bedroom to get new clothes and another gun. Definitely another gun. *Someone shot Bethany.* The last time someone had hurt Bethany, I'd...

I heard a sound come from the living room and froze. My weight shifted as I tried to lean back and see through the doorway that led into the room, and a floorboard beneath me creaked. Then more noises came from the room—rhythmic, melodic.

It was a woman's voice singing, the words echoing off the old southern walls. The lyrics were drifting through the house slower than the version of the song I knew, but the words were familiar. *Bad Mood Rising* by Creedence Clearwater Revival. Although the singer in my living room certainly wasn't John Fogerty, I knew who it was. I strode into the room and found her sitting on a couch.

"Hello, Lucile. It's been a while."

Her eyes were closed, and she seemed to be lost in the music. She rarely acknowledged me through anything but song lyrics. While she wasn't a great conversationalist, I had to say as far as hallucinations go, she was always one of my favorites. Of course, why I dream up an African-American woman who sings like an angel, I have no fucking idea. The truth was I'd missed her in my own psychotic way. Lucile was sweet, and I got the sense she looked out for me. She had a blue flower in her hair that went well with the blue and white dress she was wearing. Her appearance and harmonious being were a stark contrast to my anger, bloodstained polo, and general dishevelment. She reached the chorus of the song and leaned her head back, but kept her eyes closed.

Well, a hallucination was back. Not optimal, but not totally unexpected. At least it was a congenial one that always treated me with kindness. As an added benefit, she could carry a tune. *Okay,* I thought. *Bad Moon Rising. Be careful. I get it. No offense, Lucile, but the bullets whizzing past my head had been kind of a clue.*

"We'll catch up later, Lucile. I need to go," I said turning away.

Her face appeared inches in front of mine. I leaped back, but she somehow maintained the distance from me.

"Jesus Christ!" I said.

"He's coming!" she screamed.

"What?"

"This is the last time! He'll get inside your head. He's coming to end it all!"

She moved closer still and I kept backing up, stumbling onto the floor. When I got my bearings, she was gone.

"Lucile?"

Nothing. My heart was racing, and I'd broken a sweat. Never had she acted like that with me, and I hoped I didn't see that side of her again. And who the hell was *he*? The 9-1-1 killer? The possible drug gang enforcer I may or may not have seen snooping around outside the house? *What the hell, Lucile?*

I reset the house alarm, showered, dressed, and grabbed one of our Glocks out of the nightstand. I held the gun in my hand and felt the weight.

Someone shot Bethany.

Stop.

Control it.

Focus.

Don't lose your temper. At least not yet.

Before I'd left the hospital, Waterford had given me some basic information on Dean Hudson. I went to my laptop to see what else I could pull together. Not surprisingly, he had made generic statements at several press briefings since the killings had started. Prior to his taking the helm as the director at the communications center, he'd been a supervisor in Atlanta's communications center. I clicked on a few more links and found an article related to an Officer Dean Hudson with Atlanta PD who had been injured in the line of duty. It seemed his car had rolled over an embankment, and he had been trapped in the vehicle for an extended time before he was located and transported to a local hospital. From what I could tell, Hudson volunteered, or was *voluntold* to go to work in Atlanta's dispatch center shortly thereafter. Interesting. In my experience, there was one type of police officer who carried a level of bitterness greater than any other—those who were forced into roles that took them off the street. Usually, it was a cantankerous property officer who people dreaded having to deal with. Perhaps Hudson had been forced into the realm of communications in order to pay some penance. Or maybe I was reading way too much into it and he simply had a bad back from a car crash. Either way, I didn't like him, and now that someone took a run at Bethany and me, I didn't feel compelled to color inside the lines. Hudson was on his day off, so I'd go see what he did at night. If the opportunity presented itself, I'd take a look around his house.

As I was leaving my house, I reset the house alarm so the motion sensors inside would be active, and then I slid out onto my porch. As I closed the door, I sensed motion in the front yard and instinctively moved behind a wooden pillar while drawing my weapon. I did a quick peek out and saw a man, covered in tattoos, lunge behind my shot-up car. The man appeared to have been carrying a steel case in one hand and a gun in the other. Everything about his appearance screamed *enforcer*, and while car bombs weren't a typical method for the EEDC, I couldn't chance they hadn't evolved. Leaning out, I leveled my weapon.

"Galloway! Come out!" the man screamed with a heavy accent. Possibly Russian.

He was shifting around, using the car as cover and hesitantly raising his pistol as I tried to get a bead on him. He wasn't firing, which seemed odd. Enforcers weren't known for their overabundance of caution and conservation of bullets. This peculiarity made me pause. Having recently been screamed at by an imaginary singer, I had to ask myself if I was really engaged in an armed standoff with a killer or simply threatening my own car.

I caught more motion out of the corner of my eye and saw a couple walking down the street. Their heads turned toward my yard and honed in on the area of the Volkswagen. I saw the man grab the woman's arm and they spun and ran the opposite direction. Good enough for me.

"Galloway!" the man yelled as he peeked out over the trunk, gun raised.

I fired two rounds and he ducked back behind the vehicle. He then raised the weapon and fired rounds at the porch. Or at least *toward* the porch. I stood tall behind the pillar and hoped the old construction was solid enough to withstand a few rounds. The pillars were old, and I was sure the insides could have been rotted out from years of Georgia dampness. If the man was firing small-caliber rounds or hollow points that would impact and then subsequently expand, I might be okay.

However, it didn't matter because all of his shots went ridiculously wide, and I heard one of the windows behind me shatter. I knelt down and did a quick peek from the other side of the pillar but didn't see him. Hoping he hadn't changed positions, I once again leaned out and pointed my gun at the car. Nothing. I waited and tried to listen, as much good as that would do me after having been subjected to gunfire.

Just like one of my hallucinations, the enforcer was gone.

The Volkswagen had too many bullet holes and too few back windows to be discreet, so I drove it to a sketchy, low-budget rental car company that gave me a silver Toyota Camry that reeked of sweat and weed. I wouldn't have felt reassured my Volkswagen was safe on their lot; however, I doubted anyone would want to roll the dice by stealing a car that had been peppered by rounds. Even in Savannah, that would be considered grounds for a traffic stop.

The transmission of the hemp-mobile sounded like a bundle of dying cats as I shifted into drive and headed toward Dean Hudson's address in a neighborhood called Oakhurst. The sun set as I drove under thick trees draped with Spanish moss while continuously checking my mirrors for a tail. My stomach turned as old feelings started to rise out of graves I'd created inside myself. Sensations of anger and not belonging anywhere, with anyone; feelings I had not long before meeting Bethany were churning the soil in a cemetery I needed to keep locked up and hidden. I couldn't repeat what happened in Pittsburgh. I couldn't. They'd put me away again, and this time they would throw away the key.

This is the last time.
He'll get inside your head.
He's coming to end it all.

Jesus Christ. Get out of my head, Lucile. The Lunatic Prophecies are the last thing I need right now. I'm conducting an investigation and I have virtually *no* leads, *no* authority, my girlfriend is in the hospital, and—truth be told—the only reason I'm looking into Hudson is he's a defensive asshole. The entire city is waiting to see if tonight is one of the nights a determined killer is going to strike at exactly 9:11 PM, and this fucking car smells like a cannabis dispensary and old jockstraps!

Old Savannah transitioned into modern businesses as I drove down Abercorn and turned into Hudson's neighborhood. Most of the houses were modest, single-level structures built close together probably before the mall moved in next door. I pulled up near the corner of his street and used my phone to pull up a map with a satellite view of the area. After what seemed an eternity, my phone downloaded the image and I was able to see that Hudson's house was located at the end of a street, which afforded him as much privacy as one could get in the neighborhood. The image showed a detached garage, and I was betting, like most people in Coastal Georgia, he used his detached garage for storage rather than parking. Waterford had told me Hudson was divorced, lived alone, and drove a blue Ford pickup. So, I figured if I got close enough and saw the truck in the driveway then I'd bail on the idea. With any luck, he was still out on his boat enjoying a rare evening away from work.

I moved my hand to put the car in drive when headlights appeared behind me. I sunk low in my seat and waited while the vehicle went past my position. I let out a sigh and thanked the Slow Download gods while I watched Hudson's Ford pickup turn the corner toward his house. I'd dodged another bullet for the day, this one metaphorical.

Staying low in my seat, I contemplated my next move and decided if Hudson's home was off-limits, then I'd check out his boat. If Hudson had something to hide and harbored any concerns that his home would be searched, the boat would be a logical hiding spot. According to Waterford, it was docked at a marina on the Wilmington River. I spent a couple of minutes using my notoriously slow phone to map out a course for the marina when another set of headlights illuminated the interior of my car from behind. This car was a dark sedan, and the driver rolled past me slowly and paused briefly at the intersection where Hudson had turned. The driver, who I had been able to see and recognize, then continued on his way, having verified what he came to verify.

Well, well, well. I wasn't the only person interested in Dean Hudson.

Chapter 15

Trevor Galloway

Getting into the Bend Marina wasn't exactly like circumventing the security at Fort Knox. The gates were open to allow owners access to their boats, and the one security camera I noticed had unattached, loose wires hanging down from the back. Still, I stayed in the shadows as I walked casually toward the docks. Waterford had done some checking and discovered the name of Hudson's boat was the *Signal Twenty-Two*. I had asked what that meant, and Waterford told me it was the Atlanta police code for *Against Department Policy*. Cute.

Not a soul walked among the floating arms extending through the minuscule armada as I emerged from the darkness, doing my best to appear as if I belonged. I had no idea what Hudson's boat looked like, so I walked slow enough to read the names that were barely legible in the growing darkness. Bottles clinked and laughter erupted from a boat docked somewhere nearby. From one of the vessels, I heard Phil Collins and Genesis crank out *That's All* from a set of low-quality speakers. I reached the end of one dock, made my way back, and tried another. Nearly halfway down the second path, I realized I found success—and failure.

Sure enough, I'd found Dean Hudson's boat, the *Signal*

Twenty-Two, which for some idiotic reason, I had imagined to be a sizable craft complete with a cabin I could search. However, in front of me sat a...well, a fishing boat. There was a bench behind the wheel and an area where people could sit near the bow—at least I thought that's what one called the front of a boat—and not much else. When Hudson had said he'd live on the boat if he could, I'd stupidly thought he had a boat where it might just be possible. I rubbed the back of my neck in frustration and looked up at the stars that were appearing. If Hudson had anything to hide, I doubted it was out here. Regardless, I stepped on board and started rifling through the craft's many unlocked compartments as quickly as I could.

"Well, hello there."

I did my best to not look startled, but I'm not sure I pulled it off.

"Hi."

The thin woman was straight out an eighties commercial. She had on denim shorts, a V-neck T-shirt, and blonde hair that held half a can of hairspray. In her right hand, she dangled a cigarette and she sipped from a Coors Light can that she held in her left.

"You don't belong here," she said.

I put my hands into my jeans pockets to subconsciously convey I wasn't a threat. Fortunately, the water was calm, or I would have ended up on my face.

"Sure I do," I said.

"I know everyone in this community, sweetie, and you aren't a member."

"I'm a friend of Dean's."

She half-laughed, half-cackled and took another sip of beer. "I know that's not true."

"Why would you say that?"

"Because he's a prick and doesn't have friends."

This time, she moved the cigarette to her mouth and took a long drag. I took my hand out of my pocket and extended it to shake. All the while, it was occurring to me that this woman was *such* a cliché she might be a mental manufacturing of sorts.

"I'm Tony Witherspoon," I said warily.

She didn't reach for my hand, deepening my suspicions about her. My hallucinations could be incredibly convincing, but the one thing they weren't able to do was touch me. At least not yet. I pulled my hand back.

"Dean's a cop. You sure you want to be stealing from him?"

Keeping my voice down in case I was talking to myself, I said, "I told you, I'm a friend."

She smiled. "Men tell me a lot of things, honey."

"I bet they do."

"You want a beer?"

I didn't and I doubted she could bring me one, but I was on board with whatever would get rid of her for a few minutes.

"Sure. That would be great."

She winked. "Be right back. Oh, I'm Breanna by the way. And you said you were..."

"Tony."

"Right."

She shook her tight denim shorts down the walkway, Phil Collins crowed on, and I resumed searching the compartments on the boat. In the fourth compartment I checked, I found an envelope containing a stack of folded papers. I unfolded the papers and used the light from my phone to look at what I assumed would be useless documents pertaining to the boat's warranty or registration information. I got a glimpse of the top page before I was interrupted once again, this time more rudely.

"You're in the wrong place, buddy boy."

The voice coming from the walkway was deep, direct, and definitely not Breanna's. I turned and saw a hulking man with arms the size of fire hydrants glaring down at me. Breanna was standing beside him and she wasn't smiling anymore. The scars on the man's face advertised a history of violence. His shirt advertised a country music festival. I wasn't a fan of either of these ads.

"You're in for it now," Breanna said, flicking her cigarette into the Wilmington, its red glow somersaulting into the blackness.

"Who the fuck are you?" asked the man, another cliché if there ever was one.

"Who are you?" I asked.

"Brad," he replied curtly.

"Hi, Brad."

I tucked the envelope into the back of my jeans, killed the light on my phone while sliding it into my pocket, and then took a step out on the walkway. Even if big Brad was a hallucination, the feeling of being cornered on a boat by a gorilla made me uncomfortable.

"I'm Tony," I said. "Dean asked me to come by and pick up some things."

Breanna scoffed. "At least you remembered to give him the same fake name you gave me."

"That is my name," I said.

"What?" asked country music Brad.

Unsure what he didn't understand, I said, "Look, Dean asked me to slide by and pick up some stuff and now I'll be on my way."

I took a step forward and Brad, who was positioned on the walkway between the shore and me, widened his stance.

"Call him," he said.

"You call him," I said defiantly. "I'm late to meet up with some friends."

Brad crossed his arms. "Call him. Now."

A phantom or not, Brad was pissing me off.

Breanna edged around from his right side to his left to get a better view of me.

I said, "Man, I've had a rough couple of days and I'm really not in the mood for this."

A car pulled into the lot on shore and parked, and its headlights backlit Breanna for a moment. Feeling traces of the old rage boil up in me, I combed my fingers through my hair and looked down at the walkway in front of my shoes. No shadow. Breanna didn't cast a shadow. I glanced up at her and she gave me a knowing grin. I exhaled and let the anger subside.

"You two almost had me going," I said.

Brad looked around and Breanna shrugged.

"Now if you'll excuse me, I'll be on my way."

I stepped forward and Brad's completely real fist hit me with a hard jab in the mouth. I staggered back but somehow managed to stay on my feet and out of the river.

"Ouch," I said without emotion.

Brad chuckled. "You're crazy as a loon, aren't you, buddy boy?"

Breanna, the only hallucination on that dock, smiled, waved goodbye, turned, and strolled down the walkway, the whole while moving her hips and sipping her Coors Light.

"I need to leave now," I said, using my hand to wipe blood from my lip.

Brad cocked his head. "I tell you what, buddy boy. You give me that phone I saw in your hands and then you take a seat. I'll call the police and let them deal with you. If you behave, I won't hurt you no more."

"That's kind of you."

"I think so."

We stood in silence for several seconds. If this were the movies, I would have simply pulled out my gun, said something threatening, and Brad would have raised his hands while backing away. That's how it usually worked for Humphrey Bogart, so Hollywood mimicked those scenes and audiences ate it up. But real life is unpredictable, and real people are stupid. There was always the chance I might draw my weapon and he might refuse to budge. In which case I would then have three choices. Option one: I could shoot to kill, which I definitely didn't want to do. Brad was simply trying to stop a crime. He seemed like kind of a jerk, but he didn't deserve to die. Option two: I could shoot to wound. Of course, non-lethal shots have a way of turning lethal, and there was the not insignificant fact I didn't want to go to jail since incarceration had never agreed with me. Option three: If he saw I had a weapon and refused to move, then I'd have to put the gun away and fight him. Then knowing I had a gun, he'd undoubtedly try to take it from me, which would likely ensure the situation turned deadly for one of us.

Nope. No gun.

"I'm going through you if I have to," I said.

He took a fighting stance by placing his left foot forward, which was actually what I wanted him to do. I was good with my fists, but my skills relied heavily on quickness. The walkway was too narrow to allow either of us room to maneuver, which served to neutralize one of my strengths. Getting into a straight exchange of blows with a man who stood six-four and weighed at least two thirty wasn't my idea of a good time, so I'd have to level the playing field.

I set myself into my own fighting stance and edged toward my opponent. Brad put his fists up and bobbed up and down, making the walkway bounce. I stayed out of range of his jab and waited for his downward bob when all of his weight would be coming down and gravity would be on my side. I feigned a move with my upper body while kicking out with my right leg, striking the inside of his left kneecap. He didn't drop all the way to the surface, but I managed to close in fast and land a hard right on his jaw before he got his hands up. He was hobbled and dazed but still in the game when I brought my left foot up into his groin. To be fair, he hadn't set any ground rules. Finally, he slumped over with a groan, hit the deck, and rolled off into the water. He flailed around disoriented, an arm's reach away from the walkway. Kneeling down, I reached out and grabbed one of his wrists as it broke the surface of the water. I pulled him closer until he was able to get a firm grasp on the walkway. No need for the behemoth to drown.

"Asshole," he spat as he gurgled some water.

Some Tin Man, I thought as I walked away. *I've got a heart of gold.*

As I got in my car, I received a text message from Waterford. The message read: *Forget Hudson. I've got a lead.*

Chapter 16

Trevor Galloway

"You were on the right track," Waterford told me while we sat in his Rockwell Avenue home.

While not as massive as some of the million-dollar mansions along the same stretch, Waterford had obviously done well for himself. I hadn't responded to his text, but for some reason decided to *cold call* him at home. It didn't take me long to run down his address on the internet, especially since he hadn't moved into Savannah that long ago and real estate transactions were public record. He hadn't seemed happy to see me at first, and I thought he might have had company. However, as we spoke, I got the sense he was self-conscious about his surroundings, which were upscale for most mid-level public servants. He sipped bourbon and I drank scotch as we sat in his study. I've never really had a *study*. I wasn't sure what distinguished a *study* from an *office*, but I was definitely sitting in a *study*.

He leaned over and handed me a file. "It's a contract outfit that operates in Georgia and South Carolina—former military guys. They specialize in search and recovery, and I suspect they do muscle work on the side."

I flipped the file and found pages of information on three men: John Mays, Richard Massey, and Mark Altman. All were former Navy Seals working for a company called Trident III. Mays and Massey were in their late forties while Altman wouldn't hit his fourth decade for another month. There were no photos of the three, but the file listed Mays as an African-American and the other two as white. I looked closely at the pages, including the headers and footers, or lack thereof.

"Where did you get all this?" I asked. "These aren't law enforcement documents."

Waterford gave a shrug. "I have a few sources outside normal channels. After what you said about our killer possibly being a cop, I knew there was no way I should use traditional methods."

"Motive?"

Waterford leaned back and smiled. "I'm glad you asked. Trident III has been itching to branch out. In fact, they've bid on several contracts with both the city and the county. They've tried on several occasions to work with Savannah PD and Chatham County PD in multiple capacities, ranging from rescue operations, demolitions, and investigative consulting to hostage negotiation. One might say they have been extremely aggressive in their pursuits."

"How aggressive?"

"Over a dozen bids in the past three years."

"How many successes?"

"Zero?"

"Why?"

"A multitude of reasons. Government bidding is a convoluted process. They were underbid most of the time. Several times the proposed contract was simply pulled because the jurisdiction reassessed the need. Other times, there were other companies that had better longstanding...working relationships with the local politicians."

I could infer several things from that last statement, but I let it go.

"That's interesting, but circumstantial at best."

"What if I told you they reached out to me soon after the 9-1-1 killings started and wanted to pursue a consulting contract?"

I took another drink from my glass. "How soon?"

"The second murder."

"That *is* aggressive."

"I didn't think much of it at the time. But once you mentioned our killer could be a cop—"

"Or other first responder."

"Right. Once you said that, I started thinking about police officers and those who seem to want to be in on the action. Then I thought, what if these guys were desperate enough to cause a situation that created a need—a need for them to swoop in. Maybe they find a patsy to nail and then they become heroes and eat up the publicity…"

Waterford stopped and waved a hand.

"Now that I'm saying it out loud, it sounds ridiculous. Look at me."

He stood up, paced, and drank.

"I'm a small-time councilman trying to play detective." He stopped and looked at me. "Do you know why?"

"Do I know why…what?"

"Do you know why I'm small-time? Surely you checked me out. You're not an idiot. You have to wonder why I left Augusta and why I'm a politician who seems to avoid politician-like things."

I nodded. "I'm an inquisitive person."

"Fear. It's that simple. Fear. I've always been afraid of doing too little, so I take on the jobs nobody wants. However, I'm afraid of making the big mistake. So, I bail out before things get too risky for me. I could have been the mayor of Augusta. Did you know that? And from there, who knows? An educated black man with the right people backing him…"

He finished his drink.

"I'm a coward at heart," he said, waving a hand toward me, or, more precisely, to the file in my lap. "Here I am telling you how you should do your job."

"Not at all," I said. "This seems worth pursuing."

"You really think so?"

"Sure. Like you said, they have a motive. Obviously, they have the skills needed to commit these killings."

"Good. I mean, okay."

We didn't speak for a moment, and then I asked a question to which I already knew the answer.

"Do you want to take this to the police?"

"Not yet. These guys have tried to cultivate friendships in the departments, and I think word will get out if we let on that they might be suspects. Don't you agree?"

"Seems logical."

I put down my drink, rose, and started to walk out.

"I was thinking you might not want to confront them directly yet. Again...not trying to tell you how to do your job, but if they suspect we're on to them then they'll cover their tracks. Right?"

"Right. No need to spook them. I'll just do some checking around. Maybe some loose surveillance."

I began walking again, file in my hand.

"Oh, did you find out anything about Hudson?"

I thought about the envelope I'd taken from Hudson's boat and the papers it contained. I'd read through all of them before walking up to Waterford's doorstep.

"No. Not yet. I'll keep you posted."

I left the house and drove under a moonless sky. Glancing at the dashboard clock, I noticed it was after nine-thirty. If there had been another murder, Waterford would have received a call. Of course, as we sat in his study, he hadn't seemed too concerned his phone would ring.

Bethany was not in good spirits the next morning.

"I'm checking out of here."

Dr. Arafa, a plump man with a knack for giving attitude as good as he got, was at her bedside. He made an exasperated sound and said, "For the fifth time this morning, I'm telling you we need to keep you at least one more day to make sure you do not move around too much and cause any internal bleeding. Aside from that, there is always the risk of infection. You were shot, not bitten by a mosquito while sitting outdoors drinking a margarita."

"Most Savannah mosquitos are the size of .22 caliber bullets," she argued. "So, discharge me!"

"The bullet we dug out of you was a .40 caliber. Those rounds are larger than .22s. So, there you have it. You have to stay," he quipped in a Middle-Eastern dialect.

"Are you some kind of ammunition expert, or a doctor?" she fired back.

He waved a clipboard toward the sun-soaked window. "It's Savannah, my dear. When it rains, it rains bullets."

The doctor shot me a *good luck* look as he strode out the door past the federal marshals standing post. I scooted my uncomfortable chair closer to the bed and looked over my extremely anxious girlfriend.

"What?" she asked.

"I didn't say anything."

"No, but you're always thinking something."

"I have a lifetime of poor decision making to show as evidence to the contrary."

She glanced around the room. "Did you bring my cell phone charger?"

"It's on the table beside you."

"Oh. Thanks."

"No problem."

She watched me carefully and pressed buttons on an armrest to increase the incline of the bed.

"Something's happened with the case and you don't want to worry me about it. I know there wasn't another murder because I checked the news. So…spill."

"I went to Dean Hudson's house and I was going to take a

look around, but he came home. So, I went to his boat and found a collection of documents."

"Which were…"

"Information on all of the victims thus far. Home and work addresses, relationships to dispatchers, handwritten notes estimating police response times."

Bethany sat up and winced in pain. "You're kidding me!"

"That's not all. There was information on Sebastian Waterford as well. However, Hudson didn't have much more than we already know."

"Do you think he's a target?"

I stood up and walked to the window.

"I don't know. He doesn't fit the profile of the victims, but there's got to be a reason why Hudson has Waterford's information. If Hudson *is* the killer, maybe he thinks getting rid of Waterford will slow things down."

"It would get us off the case—officially," Bethany said.

"Hudson is potentially damaged goods," I speculated. "Let's say something happened to Hudson when he was with Atlanta PD—he got injured and ended up in communications. Later, he winds up supervising dispatchers in Chatham County. He has access to personal information on the dispatchers and he clearly doesn't want us around. But we're weak on motive. We need more information as to why he might be doing this, and I think the answer has something to do with what happened to him in Atlanta."

Bethany rubbed her wound. "Part of me hates to say it, but you have enough to take to the task force. Let them run it down. We can't take a chance on someone else getting killed or you getting hurt. They need to be watching him."

"That's the thing," I said, turning from the window. "They already are. When I was in my car near Hudson's house, Detectives Koll and Downey did a slow roll past Hudson's house. I think they have a GPS tracker on his truck and they're tailing him from a distance."

"That's great. Then they already suspect something."

"It's off," I said.

"Why?"

"Because they know him, and he knows them. He knows their faces. They have an entire task force of people who could tail him. So, why are two familiar faces, and the two people running the *entire* task force, following the 9-1-1 center director?"

Bethany didn't have an answer and neither did I.

"What did Waterford say about all this?" she asked.

"I haven't told him."

"You haven't had a chance to talk to him yet?"

"As a matter of fact, I was in his house last night."

Bethany leaned back and settled in with her confusion. "And you kept him in the dark? Why?"

I told her about the file Waterford had given me that contained the information on Trident III.

"That sounds like a promising lead as well."

"Waterford doesn't want to go to the police with it yet. He thinks the Trident III crew knows too many cops and will catch wind of the investigation."

"Where did he get the intel on them?" she asked.

"He didn't tell me."

"I'm assuming you asked."

My look told her I had.

Bethany said, "What else? I see it in your eyes. There's a big-ticket item you're holding back."

"Waterford started to play it off that the Trident III lead might be foolish and that he was being a little silly by trying to play detective on his own. He then went into quite a speech about his abundance of fear and how it consumes him—how it holds him back. To hear him tell it, he can find himself completely debilitated by fear at times."

"Waterford said this?"

"Yes."

Now it was Bethany's turn to stare out the window. I gave

her a few minutes to process everything.

"Damn," she finally said.

"Yeah."

"What's his game?"

"I'm not sure yet. But we both know that the man who walked into our office and had ice in his veins while we pointed guns at his chest is *not* paralyzed by fear."

"I have to get out of here," she said.

"Not yet you don't," I said. "Besides, I have to get up to Augusta and see what I can find out about Waterford. Then, I have to see what I can find out about Dean Hudson's time with Atlanta PD."

"And you have to do this without Chatham County PD and Savannah PD assistance."

"Until I figure out what Koll and Downey are up to, I don't have a choice."

Bethany closed her eyes for a long time, and I could tell she was thinking.

"So, Waterford is keeping the police in the dark. The police are keeping Hudson in the dark. We're reasonably sure Waterford *and* the police are keeping us in the dark. And we're keeping *everyone* including a bunch of former SEALs and the dispatch supervisor in the dark."

She opened her eyes and saw me nod confirmation. Not wanting to keep her in the dark, I let her know about my front yard shootout with the EEDC member who was trying to plant a bomb in my car. Bethany raised her good arm enough to take one hand to her temple and rubbed it in a circular motion.

"Can you let the nurse know I'm going to need more painkillers? A lot more."

Chapter 17

Trevor Galloway

I'd considered driving straight to the Municipal Building in Augusta to seek out a clerk or secretary who might be loose-lipped enough to tell me about Sebastian Waterford's mysterious departure from the city. He'd had the mayor's job all but locked up when he'd vanished to Savannah, and I didn't buy his story that he got jittery when the spotlight got too bright. However, during the drive, I decided it would be better to go another route. After all—to butcher an ancient proverb—the enemy of my deceptive client is my friend.

Cynthia Becknell was a local business owner who had expected to run against Waterford in the mayoral election prior to his departure. From the articles I'd found, she ultimately campaigned against a man the opposing party had swiftly plugged into the spot they'd assume Waterford would occupy on the ballot. Becknell, a white woman, had a commanding lead in the polls until news leaked she had once paid out a court settlement for racial discrimination related to terminating an employee in her real estate company. According to the stories, nondisclosure agreements had been put in place and records had been sealed, but somehow the news had leaked out of the courthouse. Becknell had been quoted in several publications, accusing the mayor's office and the opposing party of disseminating the information. Everything I read screamed *bitterness* and *resentment*. I needed to talk to this woman.

I pulled the rental Toyota into the parking lot of her office as a tall, impeccably dressed woman walked out of the building. She was in her late forties, wore a tight skirt and white blouse with a jacket over the top. I was impressed how fast she could stride in heels. I recognized her immediately from the company website and got out of the car to get her attention before she reached her Mercedes.

"Mrs. Becknell?"

She didn't slow for a beat but did turn her head.

"Yes."

"My name is Trevor Galloway. May I speak to you for a moment?"

She stopped, looked me up and down like a property, and seemed to approve. Then she looked at the tiny Toyota disapprovingly. "I'm sorry. I'm on my way to show a house."

"I like houses. Big ones. I'll go with you and you can show me one."

Since I rarely smile, I'm sure she wasn't sure how to take me. However, apparently I wasn't giving off a creepy vibe.

"Is that your car?"

"It's a rental."

"Where's your car?"

For whatever reason, I'm oddly good at reading people in a pinch, and something about this lady told me to pique her curiosity. She dealt with routine every day. Cynthia Becknell was someone used to hearing the same complaints and the same needs and wants from the same types of people all the time. My instincts told me she wanted…she *needed* a jolt.

"It got shot up. A couple of times, actually," I told her.

She raised an eyebrow.

"And you're looking for a house for you and your…"

"Well, I have a girlfriend. But she's a little upset with me at the moment."

"Why is that?"

"She got shot up too."

Becknell didn't seem to know whether to take me seriously and she suddenly produced a key fob. The lights of her white Mercedes beeped, and I heard the doors unlock. Becknell moved up to her driver's side door.

"Did you shoot either of these things?"

"Oh, God no," I said. Then I thought back and said, "Well, I might have hit the car, but I wasn't aiming at it."

Now her expression was wary. For some reason, a stranger approaching her and implying he had shot up his car and giving a rather weak denial about shooting his absent girlfriend was concerning her. Weird.

"Look, I'm an ex-cop, now I'm kind of a P.I."

The *kind of* in my last sentence made her raise an eyebrow.

I waved a hand. "It's complicated."

She tapped a finger on the roof of the car and stared at me.

"Mr...."

"Galloway. Call me Trevor. And I won't take up much of your time, Mrs. Becknell."

She gave me a look that was half-flirtatious, half-concerned, and *all* curious.

"It's Miss," she corrected. She pulled out a phone, snapped a photo of me and one of the Toyota, and seemed to send them to someone. "Okay, Trevor. Get in."

One might think Cynthia Becknell, having let a stranger jump in her car, would be placing herself in jeopardy. However, my guess was anyone who had ever had the misfortune of sitting in the passenger seat of any vehicle driven by her soon learned what it felt to be a victim of terror. If the real estate agent had any fear, or respect for, police, traffic intersections, collisions, or basic physics, it wasn't apparent from her driving. The GPS on her dash initially indicated we were twenty minutes away from our destination, but recalculated to fifteen, probably out of pure intimidation.

"Are you running late?" I said through gritted teeth.

She ignored the question and asked, "What is it I can do for you, Mr. *kind-of*-P.I.?"

She took a hard turn, and the wheels of the Mercedes squealed. I gripped the armrest of the passenger door hard, and I think it tried to hold my hand as well.

"You ran for mayor a while back. I wanted to ask you about the man you were supposed to run against."

She took her eyes off the road and glanced at me. Super reassuring.

"Dominique Tucker? Why? What's that prick done?"

She was referring to the man she did end up running against, the current mayor of Augusta. From what I'd read, he was only the second African-American to hold the position. A distinction that would have been held by Waterford if he wouldn't have pulled a disappearing act. I should have been clearer with my question, but the G-forces were making it hard to concentrate.

"I meant the person everyone thought would be your opponent: Sebastian Waterford."

"Oh, him," she said in a dismissive tone as her engine revved on a short straightaway. "He was on odd one, but still had no problem latching on to their social justice platform. Nothing can turn an election like victimhood, right?"

"What do you mean?"

"I mean the fix was in. *They* were going to team up and get people stirred up about something no matter how good *they* have it."

With all the *theys* Becknell was spewing, I was getting a sense of where the conversation might be going. I tried to get her focused on my client specifically.

"I read that Waterford was the presumptive candidate for the other party and some people seemed to think he would have won," I said.

She sped up with that last comment, although I hadn't thought it possible.

"What can you tell me about him?"

Becknell pressed on the brake pedal enough to take a turn down a gravel road. I wasn't even sure when we'd left the city.

"Do you play poker, Trevor?"

"No. I don't gamble, but I know how."

"I'm sure you've heard the expression, 'If you can't spot the sucker at the table in the first half-hour, then you are the sucker.'"

"Sure."

"In politics, even local politics, you try to spot the sucker at the table. You hope it's one of your opponents and you pray it's not you. When you decide to jump into a race, you're sitting at a big, round table and there are plenty of players: Republicans, Democrats, and Independents. Normal attrition weeds out the group and then, when the field narrows, you try to spot the sucker who's left."

"What kind of player do you think Waterford was?" I asked.

"Why are you asking about him?"

"He's involved in a case I'm working on in Savannah."

"What kind of case?"

"It's sensitive," was all I said.

"Is he a suspect in something?"

"No."

"But you see it, don't you? You feel it?"

"What's that?"

"You know. When all the players are eyeing their cards and spending all their time and energy sizing each other up, who's the forgotten man at the table? Who's in that other chair?"

"The dealer."

"The truth is, I would have been fine running against Sebastian Waterford. But I couldn't have been happier when he left town because I didn't want him operating the machinery of my opponent's campaign. In fact, I suspect that son of a bitch is the reason

I lost the election. Did you hear about the bullshit lawsuit that was filed against me?"

"There was something about it mentioned online."

Becknell started pointing and gesturing with her right hand while driving with her left. As she accelerated to forty-five on a snake-scribble of a road with a posted limit of twenty-five, I found this discomforting.

"I settled that lawsuit quietly years ago. I had one black—oh, I guess we're supposed to say *African-American* now—employee in my company, and I had to fire her because she couldn't do her job. The fact was, I had discerning clients who simply didn't want to deal with someone like her, so I had to let her go. Suddenly, the details of the settlement—including her sales numbers—which, yes, were as good as my other agents, but that's not the point, were leaked to the press. They had quotes from the former agent who doesn't even live around here anymore. They tracked her down in Tennessee, for God's sake!"

We took a hairpin turn and two of the car tires left the road briefly. I sympathized with their attempt to escape.

"Dominique Tucker didn't have the guts or brains to pull that off. I would bet you a year's worth of commissions that Sebastian Waterford arranged for the story to break. It was likely his final gift to the party he was abandoning."

"Why do you think he left?" I asked.

She reached over and placed a hand on my leg. "I don't know for sure, but I have a friend in the mayor's office who told me that Waterford had a visitor in the days before he announced he wouldn't be running in the election. Apparently, they had quite the argument."

"What about?"

"My friend wasn't sure, but it had something to do with him not running and Iraq."

"Iraq? That seems a far cry from an election in Augusta, Georgia."

"I don't know. Perhaps the two arguments were unrelated.

Maybe the two men served there together and were reliving glory days that weren't so glorious. Who knows? Anyway, my friend said it was the first time she'd ever heard Waterford raise his voice and, apparently, the other guy was screaming at him too. The next thing anyone knew, Sebastian Waterford was packing his bags for Savannah."

"What was the visitor's name?"

"Do you really have a girlfriend?"

I shrugged. "People say she's too young for me."

We arrived at a massive house that wasn't part of any development. It was palatial enough that I started looking at Becknell's comment about betting a year's commission that Waterford was behind the media leak in a whole new light.

"I don't remember the man's name, if I ever knew at all. However, I think he'd done some work for the county."

"He was a county employee?" I asked.

"That's not what I said. Now, my client will be here in ten minutes. How about you come in and I'll show you around and then when he gets here, I'll introduce you as my associate?" Becknell suggested.

He did work for the county, but wasn't a county employee, I thought.

Remembering Waterford's study, it had been clean and professional, just like the bios he used on websites. Sterile, almost. One thing that had been eating at me about the man was how he seemed to bury his military service as if it were an annoying afterthought that had to be mentioned although he'd rather it be forgotten. In all the years I'd been involved in law enforcement, I'd worked with dozens of people who had served in the military, and most had one thing in common: pride. They displayed patches, certificates, coins, plaques, and medals. Rarely did I come across a veteran's cubicle or office space that didn't at least hint at the resident's former role in life. But not Sebastian Waterford. Not one trinket had been visible in his study. Not a lapel pin in a display case nor an old sidearm hung on a wall. Nothing.

I pulled out my cell phone and clicked on an app.

"Hey, did you hear me?" asked the real estate agent. "I have some time after this showing. Maybe we can get lunch?"

We weren't in the city but weren't in the middle of nowhere either. The app on my phone told me an Uber driver could be at my location in fifteen minutes. I clicked an icon to let Jaymie know his services were needed immediately.

"Trevor?"

"Sorry, I have a ride coming. I need to pick up my kids," I said as I started getting out of the car.

"Kids?"

I got out of the car, and the ground under my feet had never felt so good.

"Yeah, three of them. All black—I mean *African-American*. I can bring them here if you'd like to meet them."

She didn't answer.

"Okay then."

I slammed the car door and started walking down the gravel road, leaving the crazy racist lady behind and moving a few steps closer to the truth.

Chapter 18

Trevor Galloway

While in Augusta, I decided to go ahead and make a run at a couple other people to see if I could dig up any more gossip about Sebastian Waterford. However, a political reporter at the local newspaper told me to get lost, and an administrative assistant at the Municipal Building conveyed the same sentiment, so I left town. I arrived back in Savannah early enough to pay Bethany a visit at the hospital and fill her in on what I'd learned from Cynthia Becknell. Bethany agreed with me that our client had some serious explaining to do. When a nurse came in to tell me visiting hours were ending, I spent another few minutes listening to my girlfriend complain about being stuck in the hospital before heading home to get some sleep.

    I slowed the rental car as I turned onto my street and scanned the surroundings for anything unusual. All seemed quiet, so I pulled in my driveway, made my way into the house, and deactivated the alarm. I locked up, reset the alarm, showered, threw on a pair of sweatpants and an old Pittsburgh Pirates sweatshirt, and grabbed a Sam Adams from the refrigerator. I sat down on the couch, my phone on one side and gun on the other, when my phone chimed. It was a text from Chase that read, *It's me. Don't shoot.*

I stared at the words, trying to figure out why my best friend, who should have just returned from his honeymoon, would have sent the message. It was possible he'd meant to message someone else and sent it to me in error, but it was an odd message still. The mystery became less murky when my doorbell rang.

Moving toward the door, I said, "Yes."

"Open the damn door. The mosquitos down here are killing me."

I keyed in the alarm code and let Chase in.

"What the hell are you doing here?"

"I returned from a cruise with my incredibly sexy and intelligent new bride and decided I missed seeing you," he said.

"I sense sarcasm."

"You should be a fucking detective."

"Want a beer?"

"Of course I want a beer. Where's the living room? Over there? I'll wait there."

He was sitting in a normal-size chair that seemed too small for him when I returned with his drink. I handed it to him and took my seat on the couch.

"Your gun was saving your seat for you, so I thought you might want the couch."

"You always tell me to be careful," I said.

He took a long pull from the bottle.

"Is everything all right, Chase? You're a long way from Pennsylvania."

"Two damn flights and I rented a car at the airport," he said. "I couldn't get a direct flight this time of year. What's up with that?"

I shrugged. "I would have picked you up, but I didn't know you were coming."

"And what would you have said if I told you I was coming here?"

"I would have asked *why*."

"I would have told you that I was coming to Savannah because my friend, who should be avoiding stress and who I've always looked out for, is involved in a major homicide investigation, and his girlfriend—who I happen to care about a great deal—is in the hospital with a gunshot wound. I would have added that this so-called friend had not bothered to inform me regarding any of these events and is a complete dickhead!"

"You were on a boat in the middle of the ocean," I said.

"I would have swam back if I'd known Bethany had been shot!" he snarled.

I believed him.

"Look. Things escalated quickly and there wasn't anything you could—"

"You still should have told me!"

I let the moment settle and hoped he was getting everything out of his system. When Chase got worked up, there was no talking him down.

After nearly a minute had passed, I said, "Did Bethany call you?"

"No," he barked. "I'm pissed at her too. But she's cute and sweet, so you'll get the worst of it."

I waited for him to keep talking. When he didn't, I rolled my hand in a *go ahead and tell me* gesture.

"Your name was getting bounced around Savannah PD, Chatham County PD, *and* the Georgia Bureau of Investigation."

That was all he had to say. Chase was a never-ending resource of information and seemed to know someone in every local, state, and federal law enforcement agency in the country. Once Waterford had arranged the meeting with Hudson, Downey, and Koll, news of our involvement spreading through the local task force was inevitable. If the GBI was getting involved, that was news to me, but state involvement in the case was inevitable. Regardless of jurisdiction, someone was bound to Google me and, among other things, see I was a former Pittsburgh cop. Once Pittsburgh PD was mentioned, the first name that would have come to somebody's mind was Chase Vinson, because—as I always said—everyone knew Chase.

Chase lectured me for another three minutes, finished off his beer, and finally said, "So fill me in."

"Chase. You got married a week ago. Go home and spend time with Lauren."

He shook his head. "She's back to work and has patients to see."

"She's a pediatrician," I said incredulously. "The kids with sore throats can see another doctor. Spend some time with each other."

"We're both workaholics and we agreed that a short cruise was all we could handle. Trust me. It's better this way. Now tell me about the case."

I relented and gave him all the details. He was fairly passive until I went back and mentioned the drug gang enforcer with the silver case who seemed to want to blow me up.

"Damn it. You're going to have to move again," he told me.

"Bethany has a business here. She's trying to create a life for herself."

"They are never going to stop. You know that."

I had already thought about it and knew Chase was right. Bethany and I had planned to stay and fight, but in my heart I knew there was no way we were going to be able to stay in Savannah long-term now that the EEDC had found us. Even if we took out the man with the case, they would send another, then another, then another. They could miss a hundred times, but we couldn't slip once. A war of attrition is impossible to win if you're battling unlimited resources with countless hallucinations.

"You say Waterford is sketchy on his military background and is tied to at least one of the Trident III guys?" Chase asked.

"Right."

"What branch of the military?"

"Air Force."

"Any idea where he was stationed?"

"None. Although it sounds like he served in Iraq at some point."

"How far are we from Robins Air Force Base?" Chase asked.

"I'm not positive, but I think it's less than a three-hour drive."

"Okay."

I waited. After it was obvious he wasn't going to say any more, I said, "Okay?"

"I know an Air Force OSI agent based there. I'll pay her a visit tomorrow. I've dealt with them a time or two, and the Office of Special Investigations usually knows where the bodies are buried, but if they don't, they can certainly lead you to the boneyard."

"How?"

"How what?" he asked innocently.

"How in the hell do you know someone who works for OSI in the middle of Georgia? And don't give me your usual bullshit about how you met her at some conference or a training class on forensics. You take one or two classes a year, and there is no way you've met that many people and remembered all of their names. I've been in Savannah for a year and I feel like I know two people. You can open the phone book, put your finger down, and the odds are you know the person and what food allergy they have."

"That's ridiculous," he said. "Nobody uses a phone book anymore."

"Not my point. Tell me right now how you know this woman, and," I picked up my gun and pointed it toward the ceiling, "if you tell me you had drinks with her after a seminar on clandestine drug labs, I'm going to shoot you in the knee. I'm not lying," I lied.

"Fine, fine," he said laughing. "But you're not going to believe me."

"Try me."

Chase maintained a wide grin on his face, relishing the moment.

"Camila happens to be my cousin. On my mother's side. She couldn't come to the wedding, but I should stop by anyway since I'm in the general vicinity."

I looked my large, tattooed friend over for any indication he was lying. He wasn't. I put down the gun.

"Now, can I have another beer, or will that cost me a kneecap?"

"Might as well get me one too," was all I could say.

My phone rang as he came back with the drinks. I recognized the number as being Sebastian Waterford's. At first, I wondered why he would be calling me so late in the evening, but then I checked the time. It was simple math. Five minutes for him to get the call and another one until he called me. It was 9:17 PM, and my phone ringing meant that six minutes prior something terrible had happened.

"Galloway," I said.

"You need to come to the communications center."

Waterford sounded different. He sounded legitimately shaken.

"I assume there's been another killing," I said.

He didn't respond, and I thought he might have disconnected the call, but then I heard a breath. Chase looked at me. I put the phone on speaker so he could hear.

"Sebastian. Was there another murder?" I asked.

After a pause, he answered. "Yes."

"Where is the scene? I can go directly there?"

There was some rustling and background noise on his end, and then I heard, "...communications center."

"I didn't catch that. Instead of coming to the communications center, I can—"

"It's here," he said. "I was here when the call came in. Your scene...your scene is *here*."

Chase and I arrived at the front door and approached the area where Crystal, the receptionist, had been stationed during normal business hours. She wasn't there, but I noticed her desk appeared different somehow, as if it had been rearranged. I texted Waterford and although I'd expected him to be in the building, he appeared behind us. He'd trailed us in from the parking lot.

"I needed some air," he said as he scanned a card across a reader and a thick steel door unlocked.

Waterford barely glanced at Chase, but I made introductions anyway as we walked through a series of hallways toward the sounds of conversations and police radios. The distraught county commissioner led us to one of two doorways of a kitchen that appeared to double as a staff breakroom.

"I'll be right back," said Waterford as he disappeared around a corner, presumably to go talk to someone.

In the kitchen, the body of a man in a University of Alabama T-shirt sat in a chair in front of a round table in the center of the room. His eyes were bulging in horror and his throat had been slit clear across. The victim was facing us but had his back to another entryway where the killer could have caught him by surprise.

Blood from arterial spray covered much of the floor, the table, and part of a nearby counter. A serrated hunting knife was being picked up from the middle of the table by a crime scene tech and placed into a cardboard box specially designed for preserving evidence like blood-covered edge weapons.

"What's he doing here?" asked a female voice.

I turned and saw Detective Koll who was standing beside Detective Downey. Koll wasn't happy and judging from Downey's expression, he wasn't going to go through the motions to serve up any Southern charm today. I thought I noticed Downey and Chase exchange odd glances, but the moment passed in a split second, and Downey's scowl returned.

"I still want Galloway's perspective," said Waterford, reappearing beside us.

"Out!" yelled Koll. "This is an active crime scene and now we have to log that the…"

It registered with her that there were three of us standing next to her crime scene, and she had no idea who the brick house of a man in the skintight shirt was.

"Who the hell are you?" she asked.

"I'm Chase Vinson. Pittsburgh PD," he extended a hand. "I didn't mean to cause any offense. I'm Trevor's *senior consultant*."

Oh. Now he had a title.

"I don't care who you are," she replied. "Wait. That's not true. Because I need to write that down for our records." She pulled out a notepad, and Chase helpfully made sure she got the spelling right. "Now—out, out, out!"

In the parking lot, Waterford paced as he spoke. "I'll get you the reports and crime scene photos as soon as I can. They may not want you involved, but you're involved."

"What happened here?" I asked.

"Another call, just like the others. 9:11 PM on the dot. I don't come in every evening, but I'm here two or three times per week just in case. Not that it would do any good, but...well, I figure it's better than simply waiting at home and watching the clock."

This was the closest I'd seen Waterford come to rambling. He really was rattled.

"The caller, using the same voice distortion, said, 'Are you ready for the address?' Of course, nobody stirred. You could have heard a pin drop in that room. Then he said it. He gave *this* address. It didn't make sense to me at first. I thought maybe it was a prank. Then, I started getting afraid he might attack someone in the parking lot, so I ordered a lockdown so nobody would leave."

"That was smart thinking," said Chase.

"It didn't matter," said Waterford. "He killed one of our dispatchers who had been on break."

"On break at the time when the killer might call?" I asked.

"There are standing orders for everyone to be at their stations every night at 9:11. He was supposed to return, but nobody was going to leave and search for him and possibly leave us two dispatchers short. Paul Katers was one of our few remaining veteran communication officers and had a good reputation, so everyone assumed he would be back in time."

"Nobody else left the room?" I asked.

"Not that I noticed. But I was watching the clock more than the people and, as you've seen, other county employees work here."

"But they scan in with their access cards," I said. "Ideally, there should be a record of everyone who was in this building."

"Ideally," replied Waterford. "Unless someone circumvented security, which isn't out of the realm of possibility. I've seen people prop doors open when they take a smoke break or let people behind them piggyback in through doorways after using their own cards."

It was true. Security processes were only as good as the people who were using them and, in general, people sucked.

"Who discovered the body?" asked Chase.

"Dean Hudson," said Waterford.

We all stood silently for a few seconds.

"You've got to be kidding me," I said finally.

Waterford shook his head. "After the call came in, I ordered the lockdown and told everyone to stay in place. Then, I intended for myself and Dean to search the building."

"You said *intended*," Chase observed.

"Well, Dean had been standing on the other side of the room near the other doorway a few minutes before the call came in. Then, after the call, I turned and noticed he was gone."

"So, did he leave before the call came in, during, or after?" I asked.

"I'm not sure," said Waterford.

Chase and I looked at each other.

Waterford held up a hand. "I know I said I thought the killer had an inside source, and you have your belief that the murderer might be a cop, but I really don't think Dean Hudson is capable of this. I've known him for a while. He's rough around the edges for sure. But a cold-blooded killer? I don't see it."

I had never said I thought the killer was a police officer, but everyone sure kept making that leap. However, this didn't seem like the time to fight that battle.

"Did you see Hudson after he found the body?" Chase asked.

"Yes. He's the one who took me to the breakroom. Then he got pulled away to speak with the detectives when they arrived."

"How did he look?" I asked.

"What do you mean?"

"Did he have any blood on him?" asked Chase.

"No. I didn't see any," said Waterford.

"Was he wearing the same clothes?"

"What? Yes. I think so."

Chase and I shared a dejected look. After seeing that crime scene, we knew there was no way the killer had walked out of that room without getting covered with blood. Additionally, there was a good chance that Kater's body had fallen to the floor and had to be picked up and posed in the chair. Cutting someone's throat didn't happen like it's portrayed in the movies. Victims struggle and fight, even when caught off guard. They flail around and gasp for life. In short, they don't want to die. Death is a messy enterprise, and those involved in the work never come out clean.

Chase turned to me and said, "If Hudson did slip out before the call came in, then it's possible he let someone in. Then the killer escapes before the lockdown."

That statement prompted another question from me.

I asked Waterford, "How does the lockdown actually work? This isn't a prison, and I can't imagine the fire marshal is going to let you push a button that automatically locks all the doors. So, how did you ensure nobody was going to leave?"

Waterford said, "I used a phone to get on the speakers throughout the building and announced we were in a lockdown situation and nobody was to leave. I then had one of the dispatchers contact the on-duty supervisor for the police department who had units in the area respond to the building and set up a perimeter."

Chase and I nodded in unison but didn't speak.

"Was that not correct?" asked Waterford.

"You did great," I said. "But all of that took several minutes. The killer had several minutes to get away."

Waterford cursed. "I should have had dispatchers run to each exit and take up a post. I wasn't...It was just that I..."

"You were looking out for their welfare," said Chase. "You couldn't have risked an unarmed, untrained dispatcher confronting a murderer. "You did everything you could under the circumstances."

Waterford still wasn't satisfied. "Still, I should have—"

His self-chastising was interrupted by Detective Downing exiting the building.

"I thought I might find you guys still hanging around," he said.

"We won't go back into the scene," said Waterford.

"It's all right," said Downey. His dour expression had softened. I now noticed he was carrying an evidence bag in his left hand. "It's always hard losing one of your own."

"Did you know him?" I asked.

"Just by voice," said Downey. "He was a good dispatcher."

He paused and his fingers toyed with the bag at his side. A debate seemed to be playing out in his mind.

"Should we ask, or do you want to tell us?" I said.

His mustache twitched back and forth. After a few beats, he said, "I shouldn't be telling you this, but we found something that was missed the first time we went through the back hallway. That's the hallway that would have given the killer the approach to Kater from behind, assuming he had been sitting the way we found him when he was first attacked. We found some bloody bootprints leading that way. Not sure how we missed the damned thing."

Downey held up the Ziplock bag, but it was hard to see inside it due to the dim lighting of the parking lot.

"What is it?" asked Waterford.

"A lighter. I'm no military expert," said Downey, "but I believe that's a Navy Seal emblem on there."

Waterford shot me a quick look and his meaning was clear. *Don't mention Trident III. At least not yet.*

"We gave it a quick dusting, and it doesn't appear to have any prints on it, which is weird. We'll send it to the lab anyway. It could be unrelated and something dropped by an employee days ago, but I thought I'd let you know."

"Why?" I asked.

He looked at me questioningly.

"Why are you telling us anything? It's been made pretty clear that my help isn't wanted, and your partner certainly isn't going to appreciate you sharing information with us."

"Oh, that. Well, that was all before I realized you were friends with Chase."

My head turned toward Chase who waved to me in delight.

Downey shook Chase's hand. "How long has it been? A year?"

"Two," said my friend. "IACP conference in Chicago. It's good seeing you again, Wayne."

"Unfuckingbelievable," I muttered, staring at the sky.

They ignored me.

"What in the world are you doing down here?" asked Downey.

"Trying to keep this guy out of trouble," said Chase, jutting a thumb in my direction.

"He tell you that he thinks the perp is a cop?"

"Yeah, yeah, yeah," said Chase.

"I didn't say he was neces—"

"So, are you retired now?" Downey continued.

"No, still with Pittsburgh PD. I had some time off. In fact, I just got back from my honeymoon."

"No kidding. Congratulations!"

The small talk continued for another few minutes while Waterford and I waited it out. Once the duo seemed to register my annoyance, Downey put a hand on my shoulder and asked to speak to me privately. We walked across the parking lot out of earshot of the other two.

"Hey, where are you on all this?" he asked me as we strode in and out of lighted sections of the lot.

I replied, "I'd be farther along if I could trust someone."

"And you don't trust me."

"No," I said truthfully.

Downey wasn't offended. "What if I told you I don't trust Hudson one bit, and while I don't think he killed the dispatcher, and probably not anyone else, he might be involved."

"I'd say I'd have to think you're an idiot if you didn't think those things, and I don't think you're an idiot. So, you aren't really telling me anything new."

"Well, maybe it would help if you told me what *you* had on him?"

"What makes you think I have anything on him? You shut me out, remember?"

Downey stopped and turned. I mirrored his movements.

"My partner is in there questioning Hudson now, and we'll keep going at him until he lawyers up. However, as soon as we got accusatory with him, he started talking about how he heard someone was snooping around his boat and assaulted one of his friends. Guess what kind of description Hudson's friend gave him of the snooper?"

"First," I said, "we both know there is no way Hudson has any friends. So, that part of the story is bogus. Second, if you're implying I fit the description, then I might have an alibi. What day and time did all this supposedly happen?"

He told me which date and the approximate time.

"You see," I said, "I don't remember exactly where I was at

that time. But not long before that, I was watching you and Koll tail Dean Hudson from a distance, as if you had a GPS device on his truck. Which would mean you had a strong reason to suspect he was up to something even before tonight. So, maybe you could be a little more forthcoming if you expect me to shell out information your way."

Downey looked down at the ground, and I could tell he was grinning with one side of his mouth.

"What do you know about Hudson's past?" he asked.

"He was with Atlanta PD, was in an accident, and ended up in their communications division before coming here. Not much else," I admitted.

"He's a psych case. When he rolled his car down an embankment, someone called it in but kept driving. Who knows why they didn't stick around or check on him. Maybe they were drunk or had warrants. Whatever. Anyway, the dispatcher sent units out to Simms Valley Drive. The problem was Hudson was injured off Crest Valley Drive. He couldn't reach his radio and had to lay there in excruciating pain listening to his colleagues race up and down the wrong road. It messed him up pretty bad, both mentally and physically. The doctors told him the amount of time he was pinned in that car contributed to the damage to his body. It cost him any chance he had at working the street again."

"Then they assigned him to communications?" I asked incredulously. "That's insane."

"You know how it goes in government work," said Downey. "At first, he didn't voice anger at the system. Then he expressed a desire to correct the mistakes that caused him pain. The next thing you know he's assigned to communications, but it turns out he's a head case. He quietly gets pushed out and ends up in Chatham County because nobody in Atlanta wants to say anything that would keep him from exiting the building."

"Jesus. He had records on his boat, Downey. He had info on all of the victims up to that point and their personal information. He'd estimated police response times to some of their houses." I looked back across the parking lot to where Waterford and Chase were talking. "He had information on Sebastian Waterford as well."

Now Downey was decidedly unhappy.

"You've got to give me that information. You and Waterford can't withhold evidence like that!"

"He doesn't know," I said.

"What?"

"I haven't told Waterford."

Downey calmed down. "Why not?"

I didn't answer.

Downey pointed at me and smiled. "Because you don't trust him."

"Because I don't trust him."

Downey laughed. "You don't trust the police. You don't trust your own client. From what I've heard and read about you, you can't trust yourself. Why exactly are you doing this?"

I pondered his question, which was a fair one.

"Are you good at anything else other than police work?" I asked.

"I've renovated and flipped a couple of houses. So, yeah. I guess I am."

"That's good," I said. "I'm not."

"Well, Mr. Galloway," Downey began, staring off into the darkness, "being good at being one of the good guys isn't a bad thing."

"Right," I said.

The good guys, I wondered.

Chapter 19

Trevor Galloway

Sleep should have found me quickly after I arrived home, but my mind was working overtime. Chase was snoring down the hall in the guest room, and I imagined Bethany was either sleeping fitfully or watching bad late-night television in her hospital room. While my body was exhausted, several loose threads were tickling my skin.

With Koll and Downey chasing down the Hudson angle, I decided to focus on other alternatives. If nothing else, Hudson was going to have a tough time with the detectives. I'd given Downey the information I'd taken from the boat. Of course, the packet had been obtained illegally, so I had no idea how Downey planned to use it, but he did seem like a clever fellow.

I knew the killer had to have inside knowledge and, as it appeared now, some level of physical access to the communications center. Hudson could have supplied that access, but if not him, then who? The Trident III trio had to be viewed as potential suspects. They were highly trained SEALs and had motive to create chaos, but Waterford obviously didn't want the police to know about them yet. If he was right, and Trident III did have good contacts within the law enforcement community, it was conceivable they were able to use someone who would give them access to the communications center to kill Paul Katers. Maybe I was being too hard on Waterford. My distrust of him could have been stemming from my general distrust of politicians and not anything deeper. But the acting performance he put on in his study warranted caution. I sensed something about him underneath what he allowed people to see. I suspected deep down he had the ability to pump ice through his veins and sharpen his wits to a point that could cut glass. Most politicians work hard to display strength. Sebastian Waterford had to consciously expend energy in order to show the world vulnerability.

Although I tried to not let my thoughts return to Dean Hudson, I laid in bed dwelling on the rage he must have felt being pinned in his patrol car and hearing the radio chatter of people desperately searching the wrong area. To have lost his gun and badge and have permanent physical limitations because of somebody's screw up had to have taken a toll on the man. It would on anyone. I knew better than anybody what that journey could do to a person. Something about the trail of thoughts through a forest of resentment and abandonment seemed to be going somewhere, but the breadcrumbs faded from my sight as sleep found me at last.

"Hey, you."

"Chase!"

Chase leaned down to the hospital bed and gave Bethany a hug, taking care not to squeeze her injured shoulder.

"How was the cruise?" Bethany beamed.

"It was great. I mean, being with Lauren was great. It turns out I get a little seasick, but we managed."

"You didn't have to come down here. I'm doing okay."

"What would you two have done if you'd heard I'd gotten mixed up in a major case and ended up getting myself shot?"

We didn't answer. We didn't have to.

"Anyway," he continued, "I'm here and I figured I might as

well fill in while you're recuperating."

"You know your company is always appreciated, but you won't be needed as a substitute for long. I should get my walking papers tomorrow at the latest."

"Is that what Dr. Arafa is saying, or is that what non-doctor Bethany Nolan is saying?" I asked.

She smiled broadly and said, "The good doctor and I have come to an understanding. We have agreed this hospital, and his staff in particular, will be able to return to a calmer and less aggravated state should my convalescence be permitted to continue in a home setting."

"In other words, you've bugged the hell out of him," I summarized.

"That is correct," she said with pride.

"That's my girl," said Chase, giving her a fist bump.

Bethany spent a few minutes asking Chase more questions about his short honeymoon and getting details on the cruise, in the event she and I would want to go on one—because being stuck on a boat with a bunch of strangers *and* my hallucinations sounded *super* appealing to me. Then, she asked me where I was in the case. She hadn't checked the news yet, so I had to deliver the bad news about Paul Katers being killed in the coms center.

"Oh, my God. This changes everything," she said. "He's gone from targeting families to targeting dispatchers. And he hit them right where they work."

"The police are looking at Hudson hard as a possible accomplice. They also found a lighter at the scene. It had a SEAL logo on it."

"Trident III," she said, mostly to herself. "Did you tell the police about them?"

"Not yet. Waterford didn't want to, and I'm not convinced he's wrong. If the Trident crew is involved and they are getting help from the inside, then maybe it's too early to let Downey and Koll know."

"Okay," she said. "Tell me about the scene."

I gave Bethany the details of the call, the pseudo-lockdown, and the police response. Then I moved on to the more graphic details.

"Katas was killed in the breakroom. It looks like he was attacked from behind and his throat was cut. It's likely his body was then repositioned back into the chair in which he was sitting. There was an enormous amount of blood, and Downey told us there were some bloody footprints in the back hallway. Other than the breakroom and the lighter, everything else was fairly normal."

As I said that last sentence, I realized something about it didn't ring true, but I couldn't quite figure out what it was. Something else had been off. What was it?

"What's your plan now? Trident III?" Bethany asked, bringing me back out of my thoughts.

"Yeah," I said. "At least for me. I'm going to do some loose surveillance on them."

"And I've got a cousin at Fort Stewart who might be able to give us some insight into your client. He's not available until this evening, but then he's going to meet me at the base. I understand you both have some reservations regarding Sebastian Waterford."

"You met him last night, right?" asked Bethany.

Chase said he had.

"What was your impression?"

"Honestly, last night he was hurting. Don't get me wrong. He might be a cold, calculating motherfucker on most days of the week. However, last night he struck me as someone who had just opened his bedroom window curtains to find out the enemy had planted a flag in his own backyard. Waterford was on his heels. But…"

"But what?" asked Bethany.

"But he has an awareness about him," Chase observed. "I watched Waterford when Downey pulled out that lighter. He didn't hesitate to warn Trevor off like a pitcher shaking off a catcher's sign to throw a fastball to a fastball hitter. He knows how to improvise and stay cool when it counts. I'm not saying that's a bad thing, it's simply something I noticed."

"Great. You two are running down leads and I'm still stuck here eating terrible hospital food," Bethany complained.

"You have two federal marshals right outside the door. Maybe one of them will play cards with you," I said.

"You know I never gamble," she replied flatly.

Chase snorted and we both looked at him.

Noticing we were staring at him, he looked at me and said, "I'm sorry, but she hooked up with you. I found the statement ironic."

"Anyway, we'll let you get some rest," I said to Bethany.

Bethany sighed. "All I get is rest. I can't wait to get out of here."

"Soon," I said.

Chase and I walked out of the hospital and to my rental car. After I did my usual cursory check under the car for an explosive device—something Chase found to be unnerving—we got in. The morning air held the weight of humidity, and a light drizzle had started to fall. I put the keys in the ignition, started the engine, but didn't put the car in gear. Something about the scene at the communications center was still bothering me, but I couldn't get a handle on it. I grabbed my phone and called Detective Downey who picked up on the first ring. After a couple of minutes, I'd convinced him to let Chase and me return to the communications center to take another look around.

"What are you expecting to find?" Chase asked. "By now they've gone over that place with a fine-tooth comb."

"Probably nothing," I admitted. "Downey said nothing new has been discovered at the scene, but something about the building is nagging at me. He's going to meet us there."

"I don't suppose Dean Hudson has admitted to his role as an accessory and given up his partner?" Chase asked rhetorically.

"Downey hit him with the paperwork I stole from his boat. Hudson claims he was tired of watching his dispatchers getting murdered and decided to take on the investigation himself. He documented where the victims lived, estimated the response times, and tried to figure out if there was a pattern. He was theorizing the killer might not only know the estimated response time but be monitoring the police scanner close enough that he would have some idea where the closest units would be located."

"Did Downey give you up?" Chase asked. "Did he tell Hudson he got the packet of info from you?"

I shook my head. "He told him it was found in the marina parking lot and that whoever had been on his boat probably tossed it when he realized it wasn't valuable."

Chase snorted. "Pretty weak."

"Anemic," I agreed.

"Did Hudson explain why the packet included Waterford's information?"

"He said he didn't like the way Waterford involved himself in the case. It never sat right with him. Hudson claims he researched Waterford because he doesn't trust him."

"There's a lot of that going around," said Chase.

"There sure is," said a voice from the backseat.

I nearly jumped out of the seat and my head swiveled around. Chase spun and reached for the gun on his hip.

"What?" he asked.

"Nothing," I said.

"Don't tell me nothing. What was that?"

"Lucile."

"What?"

"Lucile is in the back."

Chase scowled at me. "They're back?"

"Don't say it that way. It's not *Poltergeist*."

"Shit." Chase took a few deep breaths and drummed his fingers on the dashboard. "Isn't she the one who sings all the time?"

"She speaks in regular sentences now too, I guess."

"Oh, great," he said, with no small amount of sarcasm. "What has Lucile been saying with her expanded repertoire?"

"It's all a little vague," I said. "Someone is coming to *end it all*—or something to that effect."

"That's sweet," Chase said. He was smiling, but it wasn't a real smile. "She sings. She delivers foreboding messages regarding the apocalypse. And this is one of your *nice* hallucinations."

"I don't think it was an apocalyptic message," I corrected. "It seemed more personal."

"Well, well. That *is* good news," Chase replied in his overly calm voice. He used that voice whenever he was being mildly patronizing or sometimes when he decided to be outright condescending. "Instead of belting out Taylor Swift tunes, she's popping up and warning you of your possible demise."

"Now you're being ridiculous," I said. "Lucile would never sing a Taylor Swift song. She knows my taste. Also, she only got weird with me the one time and—"

"Trevor," Chase interrupted, rubbing a hand over his face. He suddenly looked exhausted. I hoped he slept okay in the guest bedroom. I assumed that bed was comfortable, but the truth was I'd never slept in it.

"Yeah," I answered.

"Shut the fuck up and drive."

"Right."

I put the car in gear.

"Do you want me to turn on the radio for you?" I asked. "I probably don't need it for me, because Lucile just kicked off a Whitesnake song from their *Slip of the Tongue* alb—"

"Drive!"

I drove.

Chapter 20

Bethany Nolan

"What are the doctors telling you?"

"That I should get released tomorrow," I said. "Of course, I have months of physical therapy to look forward to."

Waterford sat down in the chair nearest the window. He was in a suit that had to have cost more than anything in my closet and certainly anything in Trevor's.

"I wanted to check in on you. Everybody here treating you okay?"

I told him I was doing fine and then asked, "Did you see Trevor and Chase on the way up?"

He eyed me questioningly.

"They just left a couple of minutes ago," I explained.

"No, I must have been going up in the elevator when they were going down. I assume Trevor is looking into Trident III?"

Although Waterford was our client, I didn't want to give him too many details regarding Trevor's activities.

"Trevor filled me in on the group. Sounds like a bad bunch. Did you deal with their sort when you were in the service?"

"Me? No, I was in the Air Force. The Trident guys are ex-SEALs, which are a Navy thing."

"Jumping in cold water and blowing things up not your

thing?" I asked.

He laughed. "I was more of a boring techie. Besides, I hate the beach."

"Yet, you live minutes from the ocean."

He maintained his smile. "Go figure."

"So, what exactly did you do in the Air Force? I'm not great with computers, but I understand the general lingo."

Waterford leaned back. "I didn't mean I was in Cyber Systems Operations or anything like that. I wouldn't know the first thing about thwarting a hacker or writing code. I'm not *that* much of a techie. I was actually an air traffic controller."

"That had to be stressful."

He waved off the suggestion. "It's the unsweetened tea of specialties."

I wasn't originally from Georgia, but I had been in the state long enough to understand he meant it was an unremarkable career path.

"What about you?" he asked. "How did you end up doing this?"

"Working as a P.I.? That's tricky. I sort of fell in with Trevor while he was working a case. One thing led to another and it turned out to be right for me."

"The profession or the man?"

I smiled. "Both, I guess."

A moment of quiet passed and we listened to the sounds of the hospital rattle in from the hallway.

"I never quite know what he's thinking," Waterford finally said.

"Consider yourself lucky," I quipped. "His mind is a series of mazes and most of them seem to have no path through. Most people find it's best to maintain a safe distance and see how things play out."

"But not you?"

"Pardon me?"

"I mean...not to be too personal, but it seems you two are in love. Therefore, you're not at a safe distance."

"Oh, it's too late for me," I said. "Save yourself."

He laughed and I did my best to laugh along with him.

When we stopped laughing, he locked eyes with me and said, "I know he doesn't trust me."

Man. He sure knew how to make a moment uncomfortable. The bullet hole in my shoulder was inconvenient, sure, but this conversation was becoming *brutal*.

"You're a politician," I said. "Trevor had a bad experience with one of those a while back. I'm sure you read about it."

"No. It's a problem with me personally, and I get it." Waterford stood and stared out the window. "It's something that I've dealt with much of my life. Whether it was during my time in the military or when I tried to work with the right people and do the right things in Augusta, there is something about me that can be off-putting and disingenuous. It's a social quirk I've attempted to correct, but I've failed spectacularly and repeatedly. Throughout my life, I've placed myself in circumstances where I'm expected to share my history, thoughts, and feelings when all of that is counter to my personality."

Waterford placed his hands on the windowsill and hunched slightly.

"I have a drive to serve others, yet in my heart, I'm an introvert. I joined the Air Force but became an air traffic controller. In that position, I communicated with people all day, but—in many ways—it was the loneliest job on Earth, which was fine with me. Then I jumped into politics, but in Augusta, I was the man behind the curtain. Here, I've forced myself out of my comfort zone, but people don't have confidence in me because they can sense...almost taste my hesitation to share. They feel I'm holding something back. Something tangible. Something factual. All the while, the only things I'm holding back are the parts of myself I'm not comfortable sharing."

He stood straight, turned, and looked at me.

"I'm sorry. I'm sure you're probably questioning my words

this very minute."

I watched him for a few seconds, still unable to read his pages.

I said, "I'm going to ask you some questions, and I want the truth."

He sat back down. "Okay."

"Why did you put yourself at the front of this investigation?"

"What I told you from the start was true. I couldn't stomach the thought of people standing around waiting for someone else to act. It's that simple."

"I noticed you limp sometimes. What happened to your leg?"

Waterford glanced down at his right leg. "You noticed that? It usually only bothers me in the mornings." He tapped a hand against his thigh. "This is a superhero's fault."

"Excuse me?"

"A few years ago, I started a workout routine that involved a lot of complex movements, including box jumps. That involves jumping up from the floor onto a platform and repeating the motion over and over."

Waterford explained how he had watched videos of a famous actor who had been getting in shape for the part of a superhero perform the exercise before attempting to do it himself.

"He made the leaps seem smooth and effortless," Waterford explained. "Truth be told, I did well on the way up. However, my knee disagreed strongly with the way I jumped back down to the floor."

"Ah," I said. "And how old was this actor in the video?"

Waterford smiled. "A few years younger than me," he admitted. "Now, what else do you want to know?"

"Why did you hire us? Please don't give me that line about wanting to hire someone who didn't have ties to the police. There are plenty of reputable firms out there who rely on keeping their client's confidentiality."

"As naïve as my thinking was, that really was one of the reasons I contacted you and Trevor."

"And the other reasons?" I asked.

"It sounds ridiculous."

"Try me."

Waterford shifted in his seat. "Jealousy."

"You're going to have to explain that one."

"I'm jealous of your boyfriend."

"Oh."

Was I blushing? Did I ever blush? I guess I did because Waterford realized how I interpreted—or *mis*interpreted—his statement.

"I mean...not that you're not a beautiful girl...I mean, woman," he stammered. "You are. That's not what I meant. You're not my type. That is...you're my type, of course. I'm straight and single. It's just..."

"My mistake," I blurted out. "I'm on a lot of pain meds. What exactly did you mean?"

God, someone shoot me again.

"What I was trying to say was I had read up on Trevor and his background. There is no denying much of it is incredibly disturbing, but—and this is the embarrassing part—as I read some of the accounts, I found myself wishing I could be more like him."

I blinked several times. The painkillers must have been super strength.

I said, "Trevor was kicked out of a police department. He got a job as an investigator for Pittsburgh's District Attorney's office and was *fired* for punching one of the city's prosecutors. He's a former addict with a drug cartel on his trail. He's *killed* people. Not *one* person. Not *twos* of people. *Lots* of people. I mean...goddamnit, I love the man, but that's my cross to bear. What are *you* thinking?"

Waterford was nodding and looking nowhere in particular. "He's so...decisive."

I stared at him and waited for the punchline. There was none.

"An earthquake is decisive!" I said. "But you don't want to embrace its lifestyle!"

Now Waterford's eyes refocused on me.

"I know. I told you it's ridiculous," he said. "I suppose in many ways he's the man of action I never have been. He's been on the front lines and has used his wits to outsmart adversaries. Then, when confronted by those who mean to do him or others harm, he's never hesitated to use violence. I can't imagine the power one might feel wielding that level of confidence under stress."

I wanted to chastise Waterford more, but my hypocrisy meter was about to break. Many of the attributes he'd mentioned about Trevor had, in fact, attracted me to him. A discussion I knew I should have with a good therapist at a later date.

"Sebastian," I said, deciding we were now on a first-name basis, "Trevor has displayed certain behaviors in the past because of necessity. He's been tossed into unfortunate circumstances that were not entirely of his making. If you were hoping to hire *that* Trevor Galloway, then you missed your window."

From the expression on his face, Waterford appeared doubtful.

"I'm serious. Have you seen Trevor punch anyone since we took this case? Kill anyone? Has he run into a room and thrown people around? No. He's being calm, analytical, and he's doing much better than in the old days," I promised.

Chapter 21

Trevor Galloway

Lucile and I sang the chorus of Whitesnake's *Here I Go Again* together as a duet. She had surprised me by not singing the songs in the order they were laid out on the album but mixed them up instead. I had no idea Lucile had a shuffle mode.

"Is this the turn? This is the turn. Thank God. Turn here," said Chase, who had never shared my musical taste.

I parked the car outside the communications center, and we walked toward the front entrance.

"Is your hallucination with us?" he asked.

I turned my head. Lucile waved from the backseat.

"She stayed in the car. Did you want her to join us?"

"Nope. I just wanted to know if I should open the door for her. Chivalry and all."

"She has a good voice," I said. "I wish you could hear it."

"I'm sure she does, but it's irrelevant. Your poor taste in music trumps talent."

Chase had always been judgmental about my music. In my opinion, he threw a lot of stones for a musclebound, tattooed man who liked pop music and coddled his pet Chihuahua, ironically named Cujo.

Inside the lobby, the same receptionist as before, Crystal

Stewart, was behind the glass. Recognition shone on her face as I approached, then her eyes dropped, and she became visibly uncomfortable. I assumed her discomfort was caused by her recalling Bethany and me attempting to gain access to the building without presenting identification during our first visit. Crystal was wearing long sleeves today, so if she had any new bruises, I couldn't see them.

"Hi, Trevor Galloway and Chase Vinson," I said. "Detective Downey is supposed to meet us here."

"I'll page him. Can I get I.D. this time?"

Chase and I traded in our driver's licenses for numbered cards on lanyards that we hung around our necks. I thought about making small talk with Crystal, but she had immediately swung her chair to the side and didn't seem to be in the mood for conversation. It was human nature. She had felt uncomfortable during our first encounter, so now she associated me with unpleasant situations. She wasn't the first and I doubted she would be the last.

The metal door clicked, swung open, and Wayne Downey appeared. "Gentlemen. Come on in."

We walked down the hallways until we arrived at the location Chase and I had stood the night Paul Katers had been brutally murdered. The glass doors to the breakroom had been propped open that night but were closed and locked on this day. Brown packaging paper had been taped over the glass to keep prying eyes from gawking at the scene. I assumed the entrance on the other side was sealed off similarly. Downey confirmed this as he pulled a key out of his pocket and unlocked the door.

"Other than the body being removed and the usual evidence collection, nothing has been touched," said Downey.

He opened the door and the metallic scent of spilled blood lingered in the air. Death has a presence about it. It pauses. It loiters. Then, when it finally decides to drift away, the vacancy it leaves in its wake is palpable.

"Can we go inside a few steps?" I asked.

"Be my guest," said Downey. "Just don't tell anyone."

Instinctively, I slid both my hands into the pockets of my jeans to not be tempted to touch anything. One row of fluorescent lights over the counter was on.

I asked, "Is it okay if we turn on the rest of the lights?"

"Absolutely not," said Downey. "We have to do it like those cop shows on television and get out our flashlights even though there is a perfectly good light switch nearby that's already been dusted for prints. It will look more dramatic that way."

He reached over to a light switch and turned on the lights. I decided I liked Downey.

I took one more step forward and took in the entire scene. Every cabinet drawer, every piece of the cheap backsplash, every damaged part of the drop ceiling—they all entered my consciousness. I incorporated every item I saw the night of the murder as well. The knife, the exact position of the chair—everything. I let my gaze drop to the floor and my eyes blurred. I felt the room around me shift and implements slide into position. The dried blood on the floor and counter was pulled up into the ether as all signs of violence faded into nonexistence.

My eyes came up as Paul Katers passed inches from my shoulder on his way through the room. He chose one of the three chairs around a circular table and took a seat. He was a big man. Big enough to cause trouble for anyone who would come at him head-on. Big enough to make things difficult if he had his guard up. However, Paul Katers was just sitting there, his back to the other door; the door I'd been told led to offices and a rear exit. Katers tapped his fingers on the table and then checked his watch. He knew he needed to be back by 9:11 PM. That was the rule, and he was a pro who had to set an example. Katers looked up from his watch, and my breath caught as he stared right at me. He kept looking right...at...me. But he couldn't have seen me. Right?

Katers leaned to his left, as if he were trying to peer around me, but then I realized he was trying to peer around the door frame behind me. He checked his watch again. I noticed him tapping his foot. He knew he had to get back to his—

A dark, indistinguishable figure came through the door behind him. There was no hesitation. No words to say. In three long strides, he was behind Katers, pulling the knife across his throat. It wasn't a clean kill, if there is such a thing, and blood spurted and spilled. I watched as Katers gurgled, flailed, and fell. However, the figure simply waited for Katers's heart to stop beating, hefted the man's large frame into the chair, and positioned him at the table as if the dispatcher had simply been resting. Why? Why prop him up?

You like posing the bodies when you can. Don't you?

For control. *You like controlling the scene.*

When didn't you have control? When was it taken from you?

The figure retreated out the same door, leaving bloody footprints in the hallway. Blood drops fell from the table onto the white tile floor, creating small crimson pools that would dry up and remain for days. In a matter of seconds, all Paul Katers would ever think, feel, and be was stolen. My eyes focused on the round table as the room slowly shifted around in small, meaningful ways and what was left of Paul Katers vanished from sight.

"Can he hear me?" said a muffled voice.

"He will. Give him a second," said a voice I recognized as Chase.

"Where's his phone?" I asked.

"What?" said the first voice, which I now realized belonged to Downey.

"Katers's phone. Did he have a phone with him?"

"He left it at his station before coming in here," said Downey. "We got the password from his wife and checked his emails and texts, if that's what you're thinking. There wasn't anything suspicious."

"You're sure he didn't have it on him?" I asked.

"Of course I am," Downey replied defensively.

"What do you have?" asked Chase.

I took another step into the room. "Katers was supposed to meet someone in here. Katers was set up to be in here at the precise time. "He wasn't in here to take a break."

"What makes you think that?" asked Downey.

"The table," I said.

"Shit," said Chase, putting a hand on his head. "Of course."

Downey said, "You two want to fill me in?"

I turned to Downey. "You're a dispatcher and you're coming in here to take a five- or ten-minute break. What do you do?"

Downey shrugged. "I suppose I might sit right there and..." His mustache bent down at the sides. "Damn."

"Yeah," I said. "Maybe you get a drink from the refrigerator, eat a snack you got from the vending machine. Possibly you read a book or, these days, you toy around with your phone. But who sits at a table and does nothing? He sat there in that seat waiting for someone to come through the door the same way we walked in."

Downey stepped back out into the hallway. "This hallway is the most direct path to where the other dispatchers were. He could have been waiting for one of them. Maybe one of them set him up. In which case, we truly have an inside job."

"Let's not forget Hudson was in there and disappeared early. As was your client," Chase said, looking my direction.

"Did Hudson explain why he wasn't seen in the dispatch area when the call came in?" I asked Downey.

"He said he noticed Paul Katers wasn't back at his station and went looking for him and that's why he discovered the body in the breakroom."

"Did he see anyone else roaming around?" I asked.

"Just the dispatchers, Waterford, and a few administrative personnel," said Downey. "They've been so short-staffed here, they've had some employees come in to work extra hours whenever they can. I'll give you their names before you leave."

Chase and I moved out into the hallway with Downey, and I

asked our escort to show us where the lighter with the SEAL logo had been found. Thirty seconds later, we were moving through a back hallway. I could see an exit door at the end of the hall. Downey told us the door led out into a portion of the parking lot that wasn't monitored by cameras.

"Huh. More inside information," said Chase.

"Quite the pattern," Downey agreed.

"It's not difficult to navigate these hallways and get around the breakroom," Chase observed. "One could come from either the front or rear entrance and still get to either door of the breakroom."

"True," said Downey. "However, this back hallway sees a lot less foot traffic, and the chances of being seen by anyone are a lot less. Also, we know the killer fled this direction because of the footprints." He pointed to a partial bootprint of dried blood on the thin carpet.

Downey moved his finger in a line to a different point on the floor where the hallway angled into an office doorway that receded into the wall several inches. I moved to stand in front of the closed wooden door. A rectangular panel of glass stretched from eye level down to the middle of the doorframe, so one could see no lights were on inside.

"That office is vacant," said Downey as he came to stand beside me. "The lighter was wedged there along the doorframe." The detective indicated a dusty corner. Not exactly *in* the hallway, but certainly not concealed.

"I supposed it wouldn't be impossible to miss on the first pass," I said.

Downey made a sound of disgust. "No excuse for it. The first detective on the scene should have spotted it, and *I* sure as hell should have seen it."

I let my eyes go up to the ceiling. "Were these lights on the night you searched this hallway?" I asked Downey.

"Sure. I was joking about doing that Hollywood CSI bullshit. We'll pay the electric bill."

I took one last look up and down the hallway and then said, "I think that's all I needed to see."

Chase and I returned to the car. Once inside, Chase gave me a minute to process everything before hitting me with any questions. He knew how my brain worked, to a point.

"Let's have it," he said, breaking the silence. "What are you thinking?"

"You're not going to like it."

"I rarely do, but let me have it."

"I didn't see what I came for."

"What are you talking about? We have a good idea someone inside the communication center asked Paul Katers to meet them in the breakroom. At a minimum, you know a conspirator was in the building. That suspect list isn't that long!"

"That wasn't what I was missing. It's something else—something from a previous visit. A variable in the equation."

Chase tried to maneuver his mass to face me. No small feat in the Toyota.

"Dude. That entire building—this entire case is *variables*. You're checking your rental car for bombs because your usual ride got shot up. There's a musical phantom sitting in your backseat—"

"No, she's gone," I interjected.

Chase continued, "Someone is calling 9-1-1 to report murders he himself is committing. I'm about to go visit an Air Force base to try to dig up information on *your* client, who you don't trust. Meanwhile, there is possibly a team of ex-SEALs at the heart of this mess. Exactly what kind of neat and orderly equation are you trying to balance here, Cantor?"

Now I turned toward Chase. "Who's Cantor?"

"Cantor. Georg Cantor. The famous mathematician. He proved that real numbers are more numerous than natural numbers."

I stared at my friend, or the man I thought was my friend.

"His work is tied to the concept of the existence of an actual infinity. Essentially, it's mathematically proving the infinite can exist in time, quantification, perhaps even God. Cool stuff."

If Chase hadn't been with me in the communications center and Downey hadn't spoken with him, I would have assumed my brain was messing with me.

"What in the world have you been reading?" I asked.

He pointed a finger at me. "You need to broaden your horizons, my friend. Civil War history and spy novels will only take you so far."

"I'm going to take you to your car now."

He shrugged. I started the car and drove in silence. The sun broke through the clouds, and I wanted to let the glow of the day lighten my mood, but the daunting sensation that I was missing something vital kept jabbing something sharp into my soul.

Chapter 22

Trevor Galloway

I took Chase back to my house where his own rental car was parked. He took off toward Robins Air Force Base to meet his cousin who worked in the Office of Special Investigations. My friend took his luggage in the event he decided not to make the return trip in the evening.

With Hudson under the microscope of the task force and Chase taking a closer look at Sebastian Waterford, I decided I would check out Trident III. The official address for the company was listed on Whitemarsh Island, so I figured it wouldn't do any harm to set eyes on it from a distance. In my office, I got on my computer and pulled up a satellite view of the address. It appeared to be little more than an office in a strip mall on an isolated end of the island. In a reasonable public location, it wouldn't be too hard to surveil the spot without being noticed. I was zooming in on the strip mall when I thought I caught motion through the office doorway. Had I reset the alarm after Chase had left? I couldn't remember. Certainly, I had locked the door.

I drew my gun and listened intently. Although I couldn't be sure, I thought I heard steady breaths coming from the direction of the living room. A car passed by on the street and when the hum died down, the noises I thought I heard were gone. Weapon in front of me, I crept toward the door and edged my way into the living room. I took two steps in and then sensing a presence behind me, I spun around.

Nothing.

"Lucile?" I said.

No response.

I heard the breaths again. They were coming from within the room. They were close to me, but they weren't mine.

"Lukas?" I said, quietly.

The dead drug dealer didn't answer. The breaths stopped and my skin turned cold. I walked to the window and pulled back the curtains. Nobody carrying bombs. No drive-by shooters. Just a collection of neighbors who, like everyone else, were trying to get through an existence that doesn't make sense.

I holstered my gun, returned to my office, took another peek at the Trident III office, and jotted down the driving directions on a slip of paper. I slid the paper into my pocket alongside the list of names Downey had given me. While I hadn't had a chance to carefully examine the names, it had seemed only a few administrative personnel had been on site at the time of Paul Katers's murder.

I sent Bethany a text message letting her know I was headed to Whitemarsh Island to check out Trident III and then I headed out the door. Waterford didn't need to know what I was up to for now. I didn't expect to learn much from watching the Trident III crew from a distance, but if I learned anything meaningful, I'd fill Waterford in later.

After the...experience in my living room, being without Bethany and Chase darkened my mood. As I walked out to the car, I suddenly dreaded spending the next few hours by myself on a stakeout. As usual, I leaned down to check under my car—not entirely certain what I would be looking for—and then stood back up. Right on cue, Lucile had appeared in the passenger seat. Now she was wearing a black jacket, white shirt, and a bow tie: a far cry from her usual genteel dresses. I slid into the driver's seat and noticed she had dress pants and black shoes to complete the outfit.

"Feeling formal today, Lucile?"

She nodded, staring straight ahead.

I fired up the car and began the short fifteen-minute drive to the strip mall Trident III called home. Lucile, sensing my mood, performed *Georgia on My Mind*. She simulated playing piano on the dashboard, an act I'd never seen her do. Now I understood the outfit.

"A Ray Charles tribute?"

Lucile nodded again. Apparently, our dialogue had reverted to its usual form, which was to say it was more of a monologue on my part. By the time I turned off Route 80 onto Johnny Mercer Boulevard, she had finished up with *I'm Going Down to the River* and was deep into the piano again on *A Sentimental Blues* when I turned into the parking lot of the strip mall. As soon as I'd made the turn into the lot, I realized something was wrong.

Although it was the early afternoon, the parking lot was mostly empty. There were two late-model pickup trucks, a large black conversion van, and one black Dodge Charger in front of one unit. However, the remainder of the strip mall appeared to be deserted. Each unit had glass storefronts, and only faded outlines of lettering remained above arches and doorframes. From what I could tell, one unit had been a women's clothing store, another had been a yogurt shop. Seven more units bore traces of retail ventures gone sour, or at least of a landlord who had decided the location would be repurposed in the near future. From what I could see, the sole unit in use was marked by a small, simple wooden sign that read *Trident III*.

I parked the car at the far end of the lot behind a set of trees. The spot was at an angle where someone looking out from the Trident III unit wouldn't be likely to notice me. Lucile finished her song, wiggled her piano fingers, and took a slight bow. I pulled out a pair of binoculars I'd brought for the occasion, opened a Coke Zero, and tried to make myself comfortable.

We—or I—sat for nearly an hour before there was any sign of movement. For most of the time, the glare on the front window of the unit had made it impossible to see inside. Eventually, the sun had shifted enough that I was able to pick up some movement. Due to the vantage point I'd been forced to take when setting up, it made it difficult for me to see much of anything.

Through the binoculars, I was able to catch glimpses of two members of the team. From the photos in the file Waterford had given me, I recognized John Mays and Mark Altman. Altman's hair was longer than in his photo, which may have been taken during his Navy days. The men appeared to be unpacking boxes and organizing gear. Occasionally, Mays would turn and scribble something down on a clipboard.

Great, I thought. *I've uncovered a routine inventory operation.*

I lowered the binoculars and to Lucile, I said, "Well, what had I expected to find? Perhaps a billboard out front reading *Trident III—Home of the 9-1-1 Killer?*"

She didn't answer, not that I expected her to. However, when I turned to see if she had any reaction whatsoever, I discovered she was gone.

"Sure," I said to her, in case she could still hear me. "Ditch me on a stakeout. Worst...fake...partner...ever." I took a sip of my Coke Zero.

I stopped drinking when something moved in one of the units I'd assumed had been unoccupied. Raising the binoculars, I focused in on the third member of Trident III, Richard Massey, carrying a stack of boards. Massey's build was more wiry than the other two, who carried bulk in their biceps and shoulders. He moved from my left to right and appeared to be reaching the end of one of the units. However, he then kept walking through the dividing point where there should have been a wall separating one store from another. Massey carried the boards from one unit to the next, and then I realized the entire strip mall had been renovated so the units were no longer separated. Essentially, what had been several separate units was now one long structure. Apparently, Trident III owned more than one unit in a strip mall. They owned an entire facility, and from the looks of things, they were in the middle of completing some renovations.

I checked my watch. 3:00 PM. If Mays, Massey, and Altman left together, I'd have to decide if I was going to follow them or take a look inside their building. If they left separately, I could follow one of them, but which one? I pulled out Waterford's file again. The background information on each of the SEALs was sparse, but I couldn't expect much from a mysterious file acquired from questionable means. John Mays was married and had kids. Richard Massey was divorced, owned a house, and seemed financially stable. However, Mark Altman was single, never married, and the youngest of the group. Additionally, he had a minor criminal history in South Dakota for assault from before his Navy days. The charge had been dismissed after he'd completed an alternative sentencing program, but the original charging document had somehow made its way into the file Waterford had obtained.

Something occurred to me, an element that might make my decision easier. I peered through the binoculars again and tried to see if any alarm panels were on the walls. Because of the glare and the distance, I couldn't tell, but I decided there was a good chance a bunch of former Navy SEALs would have a top-notch security system to protect their expensive search and recovery gear, not to mention any weapons they might store on site. So, searching the building was a non-starter. Okay. Tailing Altman was my play. When you have limited resources, you place your bet on whoever has the least amount of structure in his life. On this day, I decided that man was Mark Altman.

For the next three hours, I ate granola bars, watched the men open boxes, assemble shelving, and organize furniture and storage containers into the different areas of the building. Trident III was definitely going through an expansion, and it appeared to be a relatively recent undertaking. My phone chimed and I read a text from Chase letting me know he'd arrived at Robins Air Force Base. The trip had taken longer than he'd expected, but he was already doing what he could to dig up information on Waterford's background. I sent Bethany a quick message asking her how she was doing but didn't get an immediate response. I figured the painkillers had knocked her out. I started typing out a message to Downey, asking if there were any new developments, when I noticed John Mays and Mark Altman exit the building. Richard Massey was still inside building shelves in a section of the building that had housed a sub place once upon a time.

Mays got into one of the pickup trucks and Altman into the Charger. I waited until both vehicles were nearly out of the lot and then started my car. One of the nuances with modern-day surveillance is dealing with the goddamn headlights on cars. In the old days, you had to pull a knob or flip a switch for headlights to come on. Now, many cars seemed to have daytime running lights that announce your presence the second you start the car unless you happen to have the parking brake engaged.

Before I totally lost sight of Altman, I put the car in drive. A one-man moving surveillance isn't ideal by any means, but it's not a total nightmare when the target has no reason to believe he's being watched. I figured I had a few things going for me. First, contrary to what movies and books have told society, Special Forces soldiers aren't superhuman. They are highly trained, extremely dangerous, and can be fantastically efficient, but they are human beings who miss things—like crazy pseudo-PIs surveilling them from parking lots. Second, if the lighter dropped at the communications center belonged to one of them, then they were sloppy. However, I wasn't placing a large stack of chips on that lighter for a few reasons. Third, there was a chance Altman was going home, and I had his home address in the folder. If I lost him in traffic, I could simply head there and pick up the tail at that point.

I didn't have any trouble maintaining sight of Altman's car as he headed west off the island. We passed signs directing us to Bonaventure Cemetery and I dropped back even further as I guessed where he was headed. Sure enough, the former SEAL exited off the main road and made his way to his apartment, which was only a couple of miles from my own home. Before six-thirty in the evening, the man I had hoped would be the wild card in the mix looked to be calling it a day.

Having two more granola bars and one more Coke Zero at my disposal, I decided to stick things out for a while and parked in an inconspicuous spot at the end of the street. I chose a spot where I could see his third-floor apartment door as well as his Charger, although I didn't have high hopes of seeing activity from either end.

The sun had set long ago, and I was about to pack it in when light shone at Altman's door as it opened. It was just after eight-thirty; he was headed out wearing jeans and an untucked blue and white checkered button-down shirt. I looked down at myself. *Perfect*, I thought. *Not only does he live near me, but he stole my look.* He raced down the flights of stairs, keys in hand, and leapt into the car. After backing the car out quickly, he squealed the tires and headed away from me. I started up the Toyota and slammed it into gear, taking up the pursuit.

I stayed several cars back as he got onto the Harry S. Truman Parkway and kept his speed just under seventy miles per hour. Without making it obvious, I did my best to keep up with him, although traffic was heavier than I would have expected. At one point, I had to squeeze in between two cars to get around a slow truck in the right lane. Once I made the move into the left lane, the driver of the car I'd basically cut off made his or her discontent clear by flashing high beams at me. I tilted my rearview mirror down to get the light out of my eyes and then swerved violently when I saw a set of tiny eyes looking back at me.

"Shit!" I yelled as the Toyota nearly clipped a guardrail on the left.

The little girl, who appeared to be about eight, had a lollipop in her mouth. Once I got the car steadied, I turned my head long enough to take a look at her. She had long black hair and was wearing a shirt with a unicorn made of sequins.

"Oh, come on! Who the hell are you?" I demanded.

She cocked her head. "You said a bad word."

I put my eyes back on the road and made sure Altman's taillights were still in view.

Taking quick glances into the rearview, I said, "Wait, I know you."

"Of course you do, silly."

Where did I know her from? My childhood? No. I took another look at her brown eyes.

"Did you die? Did I fail you in some way?"

"Uh-uh-uh," she said playfully. "Are we chasing a bad man?"

"I don't know."

"Are you a bad man?"

I swallowed hard.

"I don't know."

"You know what would be funny?" she giggled.

"What's that?"

"If you were the bad guy chasing the good guy. Then everything would be upside-backwards, inside-outwards."

I didn't respond. Altman got off the parkway and onto Abercorn Street. He made a few sharp turns and headed into a neighborhood near a college campus. The traffic thinned out and I was able to see Altman pull up to a curb on a darkened side street, and the lights of his Charger went dark. I parked my car on the opposite side of the street, rolled down my window, and turned off the engine. Since he'd appeared to have been in a rush, I'd expected Altman to jump out of the car, but he didn't. Instead, he simply sat in the car, his silhouette motionless.

"What are we doing?" asked the girl loudly.

"Be quiet," I whispered. I then shook my head, realizing I was telling a voice in my head to keep it down so we wouldn't be noticed by nosey neighbors.

Suddenly, the significance of the time struck me. It was just after nine o'clock.

"Son of a bitch," I muttered.

"You said a bad—"

"Yeah, yeah, yeah," I cut her off.

I checked my watch. It was nearly 9:11 PM. The bastard had rushed to get to a location so he could be ready to strike. His car door opened, and I slumped down in my seat. I saw him swivel his head, checking the street, and when he seemed certain nobody was looking, he quickly made his way across the street and between two houses.

"Stay here," I needlessly told the girl who didn't exist as I got out of the car.

Staying in the shadows, I crept through several front yards until I got to the last point I'd seen Altman. I checked my watch again. 9:08. I picked up my pace and slid in between the houses the way he had. A chain-link fence stood in front of me and I hadn't heard any noise from the fence. Only the house to my right had a door on the side, so he must have gone in there. I checked for damage on the door but didn't see any. The door had windowpanes that were covered by a blind, and there were no other windows on that side of the house. Of course, I could have tried to go around the house and peek through other windows, but it was now 9:09 and I had two minutes to stop a potential murder. I reached for the doorknob, and it wouldn't turn. I heard a noise from inside. Something metallic had hit hard on a floor, or counter, or possibly a skull, and now I heard what had to be a sound of distress coming from a woman.

I tried the knob again, but the door was locked. I took a step back, drew my gun, and kicked in the door. I immediately found myself in the kitchen standing six feet away from Mark Altman. I completely had him in a position of disadvantage—mostly because I was armed and he was not. Partially because his pants were down and he was leaning against a topless redhead who did not seem to be protesting his presence. However, judging from her scream, she did not appreciate my presence. My eyes drifted down to the floor where metal pot lay, knocked off the counter by passion, not rage.

"You said he wouldn't be back for hours," Altman said to the woman. He put his hands up and turned toward me. "Look, man. I'm sorry. Let's talk about this."

"Mark...that's not my husband," said the woman.

Now we all stared at each other. It was 9:11, but nobody in the house gave a damn.

"What do you want?" asked Altman.

What did I want? At that moment, I would have killed for a time machine.

"Her husband hired me," I lied. "He's no fool. He knows what's been going on."

They stared at me.

The woman said, "This is our first time."

"And it better be the last!" I said. "He's not going to stand for it. This is your only warning."

With that, I backed out the door, keeping my gun pointed at Altman, who still had his pants around his ankles.

Back in the car, as I drove toward home, the girl said, "I don't think that went very well."

"No, it didn't."

She giggled. I was a mile away from home when I heard sniffling.

"What's the matter?" I asked.

Nothing. I checked the mirror. I saw tears in her eyes. Now I remembered her! She wasn't someone I'd failed; she was someone I'd helped. Her name was Lexi, and I'd saved her from choking when I was a rookie police officer. I'd happened to beat the EMTs to the scene of a call of a child in distress at a playground and managed to perform the Heimlich maneuver well enough to eject a grape from Lexi's windpipe.

"I helped you," I said. "Your name is Lexi. Why are you

crying, Lexi?"

"Because you need help," she said.

"What do I need help with?"

"You've been following that man," she said.

"Yeah. That was probably a mistake."

She nodded. "It was. Because you weren't watching to see if anyone was following you."

I immediately became aware of a presence at my side and turned my head toward the passenger seat I knew had been vacant. The flash of an unshaven, deranged face I knew too well lunged at me and I heard a guttural scream. The man passed through me and at that moment, headlights appeared at the passenger side window. I heard a crash. Then everything went deathly silent.

Chapter 23

Trevor Galloway

"Every airbag in your car must have deployed," said the EMT as she worked on me in the back of the ambulance. The double doors were open and I could see the wreckage of the Toyota. The rental company had pressed me to purchase extra insurance after seeing the bullet holes in the Volkswagen I'd driven in, and I'd wisely agreed. An old Dodge was wedged against the passenger side, the driver long gone.

"The police want to get a statement, and then we'll take you to the hospital to get checked out," she said as she cleaned up a series of cuts on my head and face.

"I'm fine," I said. "No hospital."

She glared at me and wagged a finger. "Don't give me none of that macho bullshit. I'm told you were stone-cold unconscious for a while, so you may have a concussion."

"Did anyone see the other driver?" I asked.

"No. Look at that junker sitting over there," she said, referring to the Dodge that had slammed into my car. "No tags, and the steering column has been popped. It looks like someone found an old car they could hotwire and took it for a spin. I did hear one of the witnesses say it was a white dude and he started to walk up and check on you but then ran off when some other guy ran up and beat him to it."

"A white man?"

"Uh-huh. A white man with a beard."

My head ached and I knew I probably did have a concussion. The night was filled with flashing, rotating lights, and squawking radio traffic, which wasn't helping matters.

"What's your name?"

"Leslie."

"Well, thanks for waking me up, Leslie," I said.

"Oh, that wasn't me, honey. It took us a while to get here. Station #8 got the call and brought you around. I'm simply doing mop-up and transport on this one."

I squinted through the lights and saw a fire truck and a smaller rescue vehicle parked nearby. Fire Station #8 was the same one from which Bethany and I would hear sirens from our house on any given day. My eyes got used to the lights and I watched the red and white strobes on the roof of the vehicle's cab. They slowed for me, second by second, and then impossibly froze, the beams of light cutting through the night air illuminating more than I could have imagined.

"Hey, you still with me?"

There it was. I had it.

"Hey!"

"What?" I said. "Yes. I'm fine."

"The hell you are, honey. Your brain is bruised, and you just went off on an adventure with Harry Potter or some nonsense. I'm taking you to the hospital and that's that."

"I know what it was," I mumbled.

"You know what *what* was?"

"What I missed. I know what it was I missed before."

Leslie scrunched up her eyebrows and stopped working on my abrasions. "You know what? The police can get your statement at the hospital. I'm going to tell them we need to leave right now."

She hopped down out of the ambulance and wandered off

toward a police officer standing near the Toyota, which was certainly totaled. I felt my pocket for my cell phone and realized I still had it, which was a good thing. I felt my hip for my gun and realized I didn't have it, which was a bad thing. Either the firefighters or Leslie must have taken it off me and given it to the police when they were working on me. Which meant, I was about to have to answer a whole lot of questions about why I was carrying a gun registered to Bethany Nolan in a concealed manner and why I didn't possess, nor could I obtain, a concealed weapons permit. Overall, this was a bad development. Rather than wait for Leslie to return and take me to the hospital with the police in tow, I decided to explain things later. Besides, even taking the gun out of the equation, what was I going to tell the cops about the hit-and-run. *Sorry, officer. I'd been preoccupied talking to a hallucinated little girl in the back seat when I got startled by the face of deceased drug dealer Lukas Derela right before a man I suspect was the 9-1-1 killer slammed a stolen car into me.*

Nope. Nope. Nope. I slid out of the ambulance and receded into the blackness while sending a text message to Sebastian Waterford. I needed him to bring a certain person to a particular location. I didn't tell him why, but I told him it was important. He replied that he would, but that he was following up on another lead as well. I didn't know what that meant, but it didn't matter because I had solved the case. As long as he did what I asked, it was over.

Chapter 24

Bethany Nolan

"I can't find my phone."

"Don't worry about it," said Waterford. "We need to go."

"Damn it. It was here this afternoon. Do you see it anywhere?" I asked.

"Trevor's message said we need to meet him ASAP. We'll come back for your phone later."

Everybody had been trying to keep me in the hospital and now I was being ushered out like the place was on fire. Unreal.

"Did he say why we're meeting him?" I asked.

"He was a little vague, but it sounds like he has a good idea who the 9-1-1 killer is."

"Did you call him?"

"I tried, but it went straight to voicemail. He's probably driving. We better hurry," he said as he handed me a stack of clothing and pushed me into the bathroom. A minute later I was dressed and moving out the door. I noticed that the federal marshals who had been standing post outside my door were gone.

"I'm sure I need to check out."

"No time," he said. "We'll come back and I'll smooth things over with the hospital administration. I know a few people here."

Waterford was uncharacteristically nervous as we raced

through a corridor and down a set of stairs. My shoulder ached and my arm bounced around in a sling that did little to immobilize it.

"Where are we going?" I asked as we exited into the parking lot.

Waterford either didn't hear me or ignored the question as he raced ahead and opened the passenger-side car door. I slid into the seat and he slammed the door shut before darting around the hood and hopping into the driver's seat.

"I was right all along," he said as he started the engine and sped forward. "You'll see. You'll see."

Chapter 25

Trevor Galloway

I watched my Uber driver speed away. Apparently, having looked like you'd gone twelve rounds with a heavyweight boxer and then asking to be transported to a government building wasn't a way to become popular with rideshare drivers. Scanning the lot, I saw Waterford's car wasn't outside the Chatham County Communications Center. I tried calling him but got no answer. I sent him another text, but he didn't immediately reply to that one. After I'd sent him the earlier message, he'd said he didn't expect to be more than thirty minutes, but perhaps he was having trouble finding the person I needed him to grab. I decided to call Bethany to give her an update. Her phone didn't even ring and went straight to voicemail. Odd. She never turned off her phone.

Another ten minutes went by and finally my phone dinged, but it wasn't Waterford or Bethany. It was a text from Chase.

Check email NOW.

I opened my email on my phone and saw a new message from Chase. When I clicked on the message, there was no text in the body, but I did see two attachments. I clicked on the first and read what appeared to be part of a personnel file that I was sure I wasn't supposed to have access to. It was Sebastian Waterford's file with a few items regarding his training and specialties highlighted for my convenience. My stomach became queasy. I closed that attachment and opened the second one. I started sweating. I closed the document and called Wayne Downey.

"Where are you?" I asked.

"Home."

"How fast can you get to the communications center?"

"In a few minutes, if I need to be. Why?"

I told him why and who he needed to bring. He didn't argue.

Pacing back and forth on the pavement, I tried to calibrate my thinking to account for what I'd just learned. What was his next move? What was logical? What was he trained to do? I broke free of these thoughts when I realized I was still distracted by the fact Bethany hadn't answered her cell phone, so I tried calling her again with the same results. Feeling a sinking feeling in my gut, I called a number for the hospital and asked to be connected to her room.

There was a long, inauspicious pause before the voice on the other end asked, "I'm sorry, but do you have a room number?"

I gave the operator the room number.

"Sir, I don't have any information for you."

"What?"

She disconnected the call. *What the hell? Did she check out? Why?*

I stared at my phone until Downey showed up, and he wasn't alone. His colleague, Jill Koll, got out of the passenger seat. I shouldn't have been surprised because I'd asked Downey to pick up a woman, and a male detective transporting a female suspect alone can create a liability problem. Koll opened the rear door for Crystal Stewart, the receptionist. I walked over to the trio, and Koll looked at my battered face.

"What the hell happened to you?"

"Let's go inside and talk," I suggested. "Crystal's workspace will do."

Chapter 26

Bethany Nolan

"He said he would be here."

We were parked at a distance, but I could make out a small sign on the front of one of the storefronts in the old strip mall. The sign read *Trident III*.

"If he had something solid, he would have called Downey too," I said. "The entire task force would be on this place."

Waterford shrugged and started getting out of the car. "I don't know what Trevor is up to. But if he's in danger, we can't leave him hanging."

I leaned toward the driver's side. "Call Downey or Koll and tell—"

"Hold on. I'm getting a call." Waterford dug his phone out of his pocket. "Yeah, we're at the far end of the lot. Which corner? The west? Past that conversion van? Okay. Do you want me to call Downey? You sure? All right."

He put the phone away, bent at the knees so I could see him, and pointed toward a corner of the plaza.

"Trevor said there is a side door around the corner. He doesn't think anyone is around but says there is evidence inside the building. He said no police. He found something out about Downey and will explain later."

"Okay," I said, getting out of the car. "Pop your trunk."

Waterford looked stunned. "What? Why?"

"Because unless you have guns for us, I'm not going in there empty-handed. You probably at least have a tire iron or something."

He got the keys out of the ignition and pressed a button on the fob, releasing the trunk. I rooted around for a couple of minutes until I found a short tire iron.

"Okay," I said. "Do you have a weapon?"

"No. Hopefully Trevor's right and nobody is here."

Waterford started to walk toward the structure.

"And Trevor said he's on the west end of the building?"

"That's right."

With all the strength I had, I swung the tire iron at the back of Waterford's head. Unfortunately, my balance was slightly off from having one arm in a sling, and the days of taking painkillers had taken a toll on me. My attack was slow, clumsy, and I'd inhaled sharply with pain on my backswing. With a surprising amount of quickness and strength, Waterford spun, deflected the blow with one arm, and delivered a punch to my diaphragm, causing all the air to leave my lungs. The tire iron fell to the ground and Waterford kicked it away. I was down on one knee, gasping for air when I glanced up to find a gun in my face.

"I know it wasn't the cleverest of ruses, but what finally gave me away?"

It took twenty seconds for me to sputter, "West."

He nodded. "Knowing which way was which was critical for me in the military. I forget that it's not always that way for civilians, even for police, and most people don't automatically know which side of a building is the east and which is the west. Nice catch."

He maneuvered behind me and said, "Let's continue our walk, please. We're going to the side door, which happens to be on the *west* side."

I got to my feet and took a couple of strides before daring to peek around to see how far he was trailing. An amateur would be within striking distance or maybe even press the pistol to my back. Waterford was a good seven feet behind and had his finger on the trigger. *Damn.*

"Care to tell me why you're doing this?" I asked.

"Nope."

Well, then. So much for the big reveal by the James Bond villain. I really couldn't catch a break this month.

We got to the side door, which wasn't glass like the ones on the front of the storefronts. The door appeared to be metal, but the locking mechanism looked to be a standard deadbolt. If he planned on breaking into Trident III's offices, it wasn't going to take heavy lifting, but I knew an outfit like theirs would have to have an alarm system.

"Lie down on your back please, with your healthy arm under you."

I complied and watched as Waterford tucked the gun into his waistband and withdrew a small case from his jacket. He opened the case, withdrew two small tools, and went to work on the lock.

I love figuring things out, so part of me actually wanted to tell him about the likelihood of an alarm system, but having the police respond would certainly be in my favor. In less than a minute, he had turned the deadbolt. However, he hesitated in pushing the door open, which would have triggered any alarm.

He put the tools away, drew his gun, and told me to get up.

"Can you give me a hand?" I asked hopefully.

"I'm not stupid, Ms. Nolan. Please stand up."

I rolled on my side and got to my feet. "Well, what now? A little B&E to go along with assault and abduction?"

Waterford reached down with his free hand and pushed the door open, triggering the alarm. I watched his expression and it didn't change one bit. He pulled out his cell phone and appeared to type out a quick message before putting the phone away.

"After you," he said over the buzzing of the alarm.

I took several steps inside the dark room. Usually one gets a daunting feeling when they are being followed. In this case, I was struck by the oddness of having the foreboding feeling of *not* being followed. Waterford hadn't stepped into the room with me. I turned toward him, and he had the gun raised at my chest.

"I really am sorry about this," he said.

A shot rang out and then a second shot. However, I saw only one muzzle flash. I tried to reconcile the inconsistency in my mind as my legs gave out and I went horizontal. Then, I realized I was staring at Waterford who was somehow facing me in a similar pose while a set of feet were walking behind his head. North, south, east, west…up, down…none of it made sense to me. My eyes closed and I couldn't get them open. I tried, but they wouldn't open.

Chapter 27

Trevor Galloway

"Hi, Crystal," I began. "Do you remember my name?"

"Mr. Galloway," she replied sheepishly while sitting in the same chair she sat in for at least eight hours every workday. Her chair was centered in the room and she was wearing long sleeves again, although the weather called for cooler attire.

"Because we are going to be talking about some serious stuff and there are a couple of detectives here, we want to make sure there are no misunderstandings. You are *absolutely* not under arrest, but one of the detectives here will advise you of your rights. It's just a formality. If we don't do this, we can't really talk openly and clear things up. Okay?"

I stood in one corner of the area while Jill Koll mirrored my position in another, advising Crystal Stewart of her Miranda rights. Although Crystal wasn't under arrest, an attorney could certainly argue later that she was in a custodial situation and that was a technical hiccup we would need to avoid. Wayne Downey was positioned on the edge of Crystal Stewart's desk, hands folded in his lap. The detectives had been staring at the scratches and bruises on my face, which may have been working to my advantage, because it was distracting them from asking why I'd requested they drag a receptionist to her workplace in the evening.

"How have you been lately?" I asked in a level tone.

"Fine."

"That's good," I replied.

There was a pause and Crystal shifted in her seat, the plastic and metal squeaking awkwardly for a brief moment.

"Aren't you going to ask how I've been?" I asked.

She was immediately apologetic. "Oh...oh, I'm sorry. How have you been?"

"Well, I've had better weeks to tell you the truth," I said calmly. "You could have probably guessed that by looking at me." I gestured toward my face.

Build rapport.

She didn't respond.

"You see, a man tried to kill me tonight," I said.

Her eyes widened at this, but then she tried to quell the reaction.

"I'm sorry to hear that," she said.

"He crashed into me with a car. What do you think about that?"

"Was it an accident?"

"No. It was certainly intentional. Not only that, but I think he was walking up to my car to finish me off while I was unconscious, but then a bunch of people started floating around the crash site."

She nodded. "Well, that's good then. I'm glad."

"Me too, Crystal. Me too. The thing is, I think he'll do it again. And again. And again."

"Why do you think that?" She wasn't making eye contact with me anymore.

"Because he's done it before," I said. "He shot at me and my girlfriend. She got hit in the shoulder, was in the hospital for a while, and right now she's missing."

Out of the corner of my eye, I saw the detectives perk up. They didn't know if I was being truthful or running a game on

Crystal. The fact was I was being partially truthful. Bethany was missing, but I had a feeling the 9-1-1 killer had nothing to do with her disappearance.

"Let me ask you a question, Crystal. What do you think should happen to this person?"

Here was the answer that would let me know for sure if I was talking to the right person. A guilty conscience looks for—begs for—mitigation.

"I don't know."

"Just...give it a try. If you were a judge who had to decide what was going to happen to this person, what would you do?"

She rocked slightly in her chair. "I...I guess I would want to know why he did these things. If something happened to him."

There it was.

"Something like what?"

"I don't know. Something bad."

"Like maybe he was hurt before?"

She nodded with a trace of enthusiasm.

"I think he was, Crystal. I think this same person is the man who has been hurting dispatchers and their families. But I think he has a good reason. Would you like me to tell you what I think?"

"Okay."

"I think this man is trying to fix a broken system that failed him once. I think he was a hero who was trying to do his job and the system either sent him to the wrong place or abandoned him in some way. It wasn't his fault. Hell...maybe it wasn't even the dispatchers' fault. This man is fighting the *system*. How was he supposed to live with what happened to him? I'm sure he tried to tell people. I'm sure he warned people about the system, right?"

I watched her carefully. Did I see it? The slightest hint of a nod?

"Anyone who helped this man would really have no choice in the matter. Not only would he or she be trying to do the right thing, but it's possible she might be a little afraid of what would happen if she didn't help."

Provide justification for the suspect. You are an ally. Give them an out.

"I didn't—"

"Hold on. I want to hear what you have to say, but let me finish."

Don't let the suspect deny guilt. After a while, she starts to believe it.

"Do you remember the first time I was here?" I asked.

"Yes. You were with your girlfriend. I wouldn't let you in without seeing I.D."

"That's right." I pointed at her with approval. "You did your job and did it well. You showed me you're the gatekeeper here. You control access to this building and that means you have access to a lot of information, I bet. They trust you with a lot of data."

She let herself smile a little. "Sure. I guess."

"You probably have to have access to all sorts of systems in order to issue badges, right?"

"Yes."

"And do you have to grant special access to people to get into more restricted areas or sensitive files?"

"Sometimes."

I stopped and slapped my head. "Wait. That can't be right. I'm sure there's a whole section in Human Resources that handles background investigations and clearances for special access. A receptionist wouldn't have access to HR records."

"I sure do!" she said proudly. "I can see everything in the system. They gave me access so I can help new hires with their paperwork."

"Everything?" I said. "Even insurance forms?"

Now she paused, realizing she had gone too far. I quickly moved on.

"Anyway, it's good to know you're a trusted employee. Going

back to when I was up here the first time—do you know what I noticed?"

One hand unconsciously drifted toward a sleeve to pull it down.

"I noticed your desk."

"My desk? What's wrong with it?"

"Not a damn thing," I said. "It's organized, things are placed logically, and I was struck by how you made it *yours*."

"Thanks," she replied warily.

"I was back in the building a few times after that day and something has been driving me crazy. Well, crazier than usual. Want to know what that is?"

She didn't answer.

"Something in this building changed," I said. "For a while, I thought it was something in the breakroom, but that wasn't it." I looked at Downey and Koll. "Of course the Trident III lighter has been bugging me, but now I realize Waterford planted it when he moved away from Chase and me the day Paul Katers was killed, but we'll talk about that later. No, it was some other change that was getting under my skin. Any ideas, Crystal?"

The receptionist didn't move an inch.

I made a sweeping gesture. "Photos! At one point, I thought your desk had been rearranged, but you had simply removed your photos."

Downey finally chimed in. "Trevor, where are you going with this?"

"Tell them, Crystal. Tell them, or I will."

She teared up. "We broke up. I got rid of the pictures."

"You didn't break up. He told you to hide the photos in case we recognized him after he took shots at us. Crystal, I know you're afraid for yourself and your daughter. I can help you."

"We broke up!"

"Mr. Galloway," Jill Koll said impatiently while moving forward a step.

"They're together," I shot back at Koll.

I leaned down to Crystal. "I know we'll see fresh bruises if we roll up those sleeves, but nobody wants to put you through that. It's over. Is he working right now? What station?"

Downey said, "Station? You mean precinct? You said the killer was a cop?"

Glancing at Downey, I began, "I never—" but then gave up and turned back to Crystal Stewart. "Look, it's not his fault. He's fighting a system he can't beat. But your daughter needs a mother, and once you let him in to kill Paul Katers, you put everything at risk. This is your chance to redeem yourself. Where is he right now?"

Crystal began to cry in earnest and then said, "You don't understand! He's not a bad guy. Something happened and there was a delay in the call going out and then his company was sent to the wrong address. Three boys died and Ben wasn't the same after that day. When the company did finally get to the right place, Ben saw what the fire did to those kids. It changed him. He listened to the dispatch tape over and over and took his complaints up the chain. It was one of many screw-ups they've had, but this time someone died. Do you know what happened after Ben raised hell? Nothing. Not a damn thing. Not a single dispatcher was punished, the same system stayed in place, and Benjamin Calendro was told to keep his mouth shut!"

"Where is he, Crystal?"

She leaned forward and put her head in her hands. "Everyone needs to stop asking me that!"

I exchanged looks with Koll and Downey.

"What do you mean, Crystal?" I asked. "Who else was looking for Ben?"

"It doesn't matter," she mumbled. "He probably found Ben by now, which means Ben killed him too."

"Who?" I yelled.

She didn't answer.

I thought for a few seconds. My mind raced as I tried to think of who else might be tracing a path similar to the one I was walking. There was only one possibility.

I locked eyes with Downey. "Are you still watching Hudson?"

Downey snatched his phone and made a call. I heard him say, "I know it's not protocol, but go knock on the damned door!"

A couple of minutes passed before an expression of dejection fell over Downey's face and he disconnected the call. "No answer at the front door. A back door was unlocked. The house is empty. It looks like he slipped out. He could have borrowed a car from a neighbor on the adjacent street or caught an Uber."

"What did you tell Hudson?" I asked Crystal.

"Do you promise I'll keep my daughter?"

"I'll do everything I can," I lied.

"I told Hudson that Ben knew about the information you found on his boat."

"So?" I prompted.

"I told Hudson that Ben was headed to the boat. Then I told Ben that Hudson would be at the marina looking for him."

A proud, dumb expression crossed over her face. As if coming up with the plan to set Hudson up for the kill was an accomplishment to brag about.

"See?" she asked. "Now will you help me?"

"When was this?" asked Koll.

Crystal looked over to her. "I don't know. Right before you picked me up, I think."

"I've got her," said Downey, pointing to Crystal. "You two go. I'll get a female officer in here to help me with her."

"Can I go now?" asked Crystal.

I heard the rattle of Downey's handcuffs as Koll and I ran out the door.

Chapter 28

Bethany Nolan

When I was fifteen, Bobby Brunner broke up with me on my birthday, which happened to be the same week I had to get braces. I thought Bobby was the love of my life, but it turned out he was more interested in a cheerleader named Shonte Donahue. At the time, I thought that would surely be the most devastating few days of my life. If I could have gone back in time, I would have let my teenage self know that being shot twice in the same week was *significantly* worse.

I pressed my hand against the wound on my side and propped myself up against a wall. The buzzing of the alarm stopped, my eyes adjusted to the darkness, and I heard breathing coming from beside me. A light flicked on, revealing I was in a room with no windows. Judging from the puddle of blood on the floor and the trail I'd made while scooting over to the wall, I was in the same room I'd walked into when Waterford had shot me.

Turning to my left, I saw Sebastian Waterford slumped beside me. He was awake, bleeding from his left side, and appeared to be in a lot of pain. I was piecing things together slowly. I'd heard two gunshots but had seen his muzzle flash during the second shot. Waterford had been shot first, which had thrown off his aim, which was the only reason I was still alive. As to the question as to who shot Waterford, that answer came in the form of footsteps I heard on the far side of the room. I swiveled my head slowly and looked up at the black man holding a gun. Former SEAL and current Trident III member John Mays looked like his file photo—serious. His navy blue polo shirt had a simple yellow trident symbol over the left breast.

"Who are you?" he asked.

"Bethany Nolan. This man," I nodded toward Waterford, "abducted and shot me. I need you to call the police. People will be looking for me."

"It's over, John," Waterford sputtered. "She's a P.I. that I hired. She knows everything."

Mays walked over to Waterford and squatted down in front of him. Waterford was cringing in pain and dripping with sweat.

Mays said, "You shot the P.I. you hired? What sense does that make?"

"She got greedy. Decided to blackmail me. Wanted to blackmail all of us. It had to be done," Waterford said.

"Hey, I don't know what the hell he's talking about," I interjected. "He hired me to investigate the 9-1-1 killings. I don't know a damn thing about any blackmail."

"Shut up," shot Mays. Then, turning back to Waterford, "The police aren't coming. I told the alarm company it was a false alarm. However, I did call Rick and Mark, and they are on the way here. Once they arrive, we are going to sort all of this out. That is, if you don't bleed out first."

"Excuse me," I said. "I'm bleeding too! All I know is Waterford said you and your buddies might be tied to the 9-1-1 killings, and the next thing I know he's led me here. If I die, you'll be on the hook for it."

"He's done worse than that," said Waterford. "What's one more body, right?"

Mays stared him down. "The guys will be here soon. Then we're going to have a serious discussion." He glared at me. "All of us." He rummaged through Waterford's pockets, pulling out two cell phones and the lockpick set. I recognized one of the phones as mine. Waterford must have swiped it when he'd visited me in the hospital and I wasn't looking. Mays then searched me and seemed satisfied I wasn't armed. The muscular man backed away and then paced the concrete floor. By the looks of things, I guessed the room had been a storage room or stockroom for whatever business had occupied the space before Trident III moved in. Other than the door to the outside, there was a doorway that I guessed led to the main interior area—the official Trident III office space. The interior door looked solid and had a heavy lock on it. If the lock was engaged, there was no quick escape through that doorway. Of course, with my wounded shoulder and now a fresh hole in my side, I wasn't sure how fast I could move anyway.

Mays continued tracing a path like a leopard that's been told dinner has been delayed. He gripped and regripped the Sig Sauer P226 in his right hand. I saw he'd tucked Waterford's pistol into the back of his black BDU's. "How did you know we were here?" Waterford asked.

Mays stopped pacing. "What?"

Waterford coughed. "I thought the place was empty. No lights."

"You've gotten sloppy, Sebastian. We own the entire strip mall. I was coming out of a back room on the other end when I saw you two walking across the lot."

"Wait," I said. "Why am I getting the feeling you two have a relationship?"

"You know we do," Waterford said. "It's too late to play games now."

"What are you talking about?" I asked.

"I told you everything," Waterford insisted. "I go way back with John, Rick, and Mark. Way back." He lifted his head. "Isn't that right, John?"

Mays shot him a look of disgust.

"Come on," Waterford said, fighting off another wave of

pain. "You remember, John. Who called in the lightning for you, John? Who was it?"

Mays didn't speak. Waterford closed his eyes.

"Thunder *and* lightning—on demand. Can you still smell the smoke, John? Is it still in your nostrils? Does it ever leave your lungs? Does the sting ever wash away from your eyes?"

Mays turned away and neither of the men spoke for a long time.

Chapter 29

Trevor Galloway

Jill Koll parked her car outside the marina gates, and we entered on foot. There was no music; this time, the only sounds were gentle splashes against the sides of the boats. A slight breeze picked up, and pine straw floated down from a nearby tree as we rounded the corner of the main office and approached the docks.

I pointed. "Hudson's boat is over there."

We peered out into the night and saw two figures standing on the dock next to the boat. Dean Hudson was facing our direction and the other man had his back to us.

Koll whispered, "Hudson must have identified Crystal Stewart by narrowing down who had access to HR information. Once someone let the killer into the building to murder Paul Katas, he figured out Crystal was in the building that night so she must have been the accomplice. Since we were grilling him pretty hard, he wouldn't have felt comfortable coming to us unless he had something concrete."

"I can't see Calendro's hands," I said. "He might be armed, and there's no clear approach. If Hudson lets on that we're approaching, Calendro may kill him."

Koll made a quick call for backup and then drew her weapon. "Well, let's hope Hudson plays it cool."

We stepped forward, Koll with her pistol and me with my hopes and prayers. I started to ask Koll if she wanted to trade with me, but then I remembered I'm not funny and she didn't seem like she had much of a sense of humor anyway.

The two of us made it to the foot of the dock when Hudson stepped into his boat. Hudson moved tentatively, edging his way onto the craft. He raised his eyes while trying to maintain his balance, and that's when he spotted us. To his credit, Hudson quickly looked away and said something to Calendro, trying to distract him, but the other man had noticed Hudson's attention had been focused on the end of the dock. That was when Calendro turned, and I caught sight of the gun in his hand.

Koll spotted the gun as well and started yelling commands. "Police! Drop the gun now!"

Calendro fired a shot that went over our heads. Koll returned one shot that missed and then her target leapt into the boat with Hudson. We were fifteen yards away and tried to move closer, but he fired another three shots and we hit the ground.

"Hudson's too close to him," Koll said. "I can't risk hitting him."

Another shot rang out and ricocheted off the ground near me. My hopes and prayers were becoming less effective. I'd gotten a glimpse of Calendro's face and he was definitely the same bearded firefighter I'd seen in the photos on Crystal Stewart's desk.

"We can't stay here," I said.

I heard an engine come to life and I popped my head up.

"That's the boat," said Koll. "He's taking Hudson out on the boat."

I raised my head higher and saw Hudson at the helm of the boat with Calendro standing beside him, a gun to the communications supervisor's head. Koll was back on her phone, calling for air and marine support as the boat started moving toward the end of the pier.

I didn't like Dean Hudson. In the few interactions I'd had

with the man, he'd been repellent at best. If our roles had been reversed, I doubt he would have risked anything to save me. However, he did care about his employees and was obviously determined to stop the killings, even if that meant putting himself in danger.

Damn it.

I got to my feet and sprinted down the length of the dock. Koll shouted something, but the words got lost beneath the sounds of the wind in my ears and the humming of the boat's engine. My feet felt light and I'm not sure I'd ever moved as fast in my life as I sprinted down the narrow walkway floating on the water.

Calendro spotted me when I was halfway to the end and fired a shot that went wide. The boat was several feet away from the end of the dock when I was near the end. I heard another shot and that one zipped past my ear. With my hope, prayers, and stupidity, I leapt out over the water and saw the firefighter level his pistol directly at my chest while I seemed to hang in midair.

Click.

A six-shot revolver.

I landed in the middle of the craft and made myself drop low to keep my momentum from carrying me overboard. Before I could get myself upright, Calendro was on me. As I struggled with my assailant, I saw motion behind him and then heard a splash as Hudson jumped overboard to get to safety. *Thanks for the assist, buddy.*

Calendro delivered a strong right to my face and then got his hands around my throat. I fought the instinct to grab his hands and pressed my thumbs into his eyes. He released his grip and leaned back enough for me to gain some leverage and turn over on my side. I kept my thumbs in his eyes and he held on to my hands, struggling to pull them away as we both got to our feet. I saw motion to my side and saw Koll running down the dock, gun in hand.

I pressed harder into the man's skull, but he took two steps back and was able to relieve the pressure enough to slide my thumbs off his face. He then caught me with a knee to the outside of my thigh. We exchanged a couple of punches and then I got him into a chokehold just as he managed to catapult us off the boat and into the river. I fought to keep my arm around his throat as our heads went underneath the surface of the water. My lungs caught fire as he kicked and thrashed, struggling for air.

He killed all of those people. Those poor people.

I squeezed harder.

Good people. Innocent people. Most of whom, their only crime was caring about someone who worked at the communications center.

I squeezed harder.

A grandmother. Kids.

I squeezed harder.

"You know what would be funny?" the hallucinated little girl in the backseat of my car had said. "If you were the bad guy chasing the good guy. Then everything would be upside-backwards, inside-outwards."

"If you were the bad guy…"

Calendro was barely fighting, if at all.

The bad guy.

I loosened my grip, kicked my legs, and pulled him to the surface. As I oriented myself and pushed Calendro toward one of the piers, I noticed several people were now lining up and dangling hands in an effort to help me. Someone pulled Calendro away and he rose out of my sight. I was overcome with exhaustion and struggled to reach any of the outstretched hands. When I tried to extend my arm, my head went underwater and I didn't think I was going to be able to come back up. Suddenly, I felt something grab the back of my shirt and then two massive arms hooked me under my armpits. It seemed I was floating in space and then I was being placed down on a walkway. I looked up and saw big, bad, country music–loving Brad staring down at me. Apparently, my good deed of pulling him to the pier after knocking him into the river had earned me a marker at the Good Karma Casino.

"Thanks," I said.

"You're still an asshole," he said before edging his way past a few people.

But I'm trying, I thought.

I sat up, scanned the area, and saw Koll putting cuffs on Calendro. Since handcuffing corpses isn't normal police procedure, I took that as a sign he was still alive.

That was it. It was over. Except there was one big problem remaining. I reached into my pocket and found my phone was still on me. I checked to see if it was still working and frantically pressed buttons to see if I had any texts from Bethany or Waterford. The Wilmington River hadn't done my phone any favors, and there was a scattering of random symbols on my screen, along with a large gray blob across the middle.

It looked like I did have a text from Waterford. The first line was missing completely. The second line was there, but many of the letters were replaced with random symbols or missing. The line read: *I *hi k t#e) h>>: her. I'% sorry.*

I cycled through the possibilities.

I think they have her?

I think they hurt her?

A third line appeared below the second. It read: *H($ry. She >ay $e d(ad.*

She may be dead.

My body was engulfed in flames. Where was he? What was Waterford up to? Had he or someone else hurt Bethany?

I got to my feet, stared out to the water, and let my eyes unfocus. I found myself standing in Bethany's hospital room. Waterford was there and he was telling her she needed to check out and go with him. She's asking where they are going. He's saying they have to go, because...because I need help. Of course! But he didn't bring her to the communications center like I'd asked him.

I'm still standing in the room, watching Bethany gather up her things, thinking I need her help. Waterford's probably taken her phone without her knowing it. Now I'm checking my phone, before I drowned it in the river, and I'm looking at the documents Chase sent me. I'm reading the Air Force personnel file of Sebastian Waterford, who was *anything* but your typical Airman. I'm looking at the file of a Combat Controller specialist who trained as a one-man attachment to other military branches' Special Forces teams. I'm reviewing the file of a man who trained with every elite unit in the country, marked targets, and called in air support for combat operations. More importantly, I'm reviewing the file of a man who worked with a SEAL team consisting of John Mays, Richard Massey, and Mark Altman, currently of Trident III. Not only that, but the other report Chase has sent me tells an interesting story regarding Waterford and the Trident III group.

I think they have her.

That was his text. *They* have her.

Waterford must have told Bethany I was on to something with Trident III and needed her help. That's the only reason she would have gone alone with him without question. And after reading the report Chase had sent, I had a hunch why he wanted to lure me to Trident III as well. If Bethany was where I thought she was, and I brought along a parade of patrol cars, I could detonate a powder keg. Waterford wanted to draw me into *his* war—onto *his* battlefield. The hospital wouldn't tell me anything because they didn't know where Bethany—a woman who had been under protection—was. I knew now she'd been taken by the man who'd promised to protect her.

Okay, Sebastian. Let's play.

I didn't have a car or a gun. First thing's first. My eyes drifted to the parking lot where several Savannah PD cars, including a few unmarked ones, had pulled in. The officers and detectives were making their way down the docks and talking to the onlookers.

Fine, then, I thought. *Time to be a cop one more fucking time.*

Chapter 30

Bethany Nolan

The sharp ringing of the phone echoed off the hard walls. The sound caused me to jerk and I felt like electricity shot into the hole in my side as I bit my lip, trying not to yell out. Mays reached into one of his trillion pockets and found a phone.

He gave us a sideways glance and said, "No change. Waterford and the girl."

Mays paused, listening to the person on the other end of the call. Then he said, "Wait one."

The man then turned to face us and pointed his gun at the interior door. "That door is locked." He then gestured toward the area where he was standing. "If either of you stick your head out this door, I'll place a round in the center of your forehead." Leaving us with that pleasant imagery, he stepped outside.

Not being the trusting type, I willed my body to stand—if you could call the position I got into a stance—and hobbled over to the interior door. I tried the steel knob. It was, in fact, locked. I looked around the room for anything that could be used as a weapon and came up empty. I stumbled during my search and fell hard on the floor but managed to drag myself over to my original spot.

I shifted my body and said to Waterford, "What the hell is

going on? What's your history with these guys?"

Waterford didn't say anything for a long moment. I started to think he was going to ignore me, but then he said, "We served together in Iraq."

"You said you were an Air Traffic Controller in the Air Force. What would you be doing with these guys?"

He breathed deeply and closed his eyes. "I may have oversimplified my job description."

"Unsimplify it," I demanded.

Waterford opened his eyes and let his head fall my direction so he could see me as he spoke. "I was a Combat Controller."

"Which means?"

He coughed and said, "Which means I was the Air Force version of special operations. While I was trained in air traffic control, I was given advanced training in infiltration, survival, navigation, demolitions, and the use of an assortment of weapons."

He coughed again and it took him several seconds to regain his composure.

After a false start, Waterford began again. "We would be assigned to the Special Forces teams of other branches, so we had to be trained to work with all of them. Combat Controllers are often the ones who mark targets, communicate for air support, and call in the strike."

"You worked with SEALs," I said.

"SEALs, Army Rangers, Delta...I worked with lots of units over the years. But yes. I worked with the team that included Mays, Massey, and Altman."

I looked down at the floor. The pool of blood next to him was slightly bigger than the one next to me.

"It doesn't seem you parted on good terms with their team," I said.

Waterford made a noise that under better circumstances might have sounded like a chuckle. "Not exactly. We were running an operation in a town not far from Tikrit. Although Tikrit was bustling with activity, intelligence indicated this place might have a cache of weapons that was lightly guarded. Reports were the enemy would try to relocate the weapons. Our mission..." he trailed off and closed his eyes.

"Your mission?" I said loudly.

He opened his eyes. "Our mission...the mission was to mark the target when it started leaving the population center so it could be destroyed. Simple."

"Why do I get the feeling things didn't go as planned?" I asked.

"They did," said Waterford. "Until they didn't. The team was spread out in the hills above the town and I ended up with Mays, Massey, Altman, and Lance McKay. The five of us stumbled upon a small pocket of deserters from Saddam Hussein's army. They thought we were going to kill them, so they started telling us all about the cache of weapons and when the supply trucks were arriving to take them away."

"Sounds helpful," I said.

"Extremely. Then they told us about the money."

I waited.

"Stacks of U.S. currency were squirreled away in a building next to where the weapons were being stored. The regime had been stockpiling it for years in various places in order to stabilize the economy whenever the need arose. Most of the money had been removed from the location already, but there was still a nice sum remaining."

I asked, "How nice?"

He didn't answer and his eyes were closed again. I started to repeat the question, but then he replied softly.

"Around a million dollars."

Waterford didn't speak for a few moments and I found myself worrying John Mays might burst back into the room and shoot us, having received some order from whomever he was speaking to on the phone. However, either the conversation was lengthy or Mays was waiting outside for company to arrive.

"Altman was the first to suggest it, although most of us played it off as a joke. That night, the talk became hypothetical. Then, it turned real. All of that money, tax-free. Who would know? Who would care? We knew how people felt about us being over there this time around. Hell, most of us didn't want to be over there. All of us were hearing nightmare stories about the big lie the military tells you." Waterford transitioned into a mocking, radio announcer–like voice and I thought he might have gone delirious. "We'll help you transition over to civilian life. Get you the training you need. You'll land a job in no time because people love to hire vets."

He coughed again and wheezed. "We knew there were real possibilities that we could end up fighting the VA to get medical treatment because we breathed in so much smoke from the oil fields or took shrapnel from an IED. People we knew had drained their families' bank accounts trying to get right after serving overseas. Most of us decided that wasn't going to be us. When we got back home, we were going to be a few rungs up on the ladder. We'd have startup money or a nest egg to fall back on."

"You took the money," I said. "That's why you live so well. I guess the others used the money to start up Trident III."

Waterford raised a hand and wiped his brow.

"They ran through their money and pressured me to throw them business when I was in Augusta. I never wanted to be mayor. When I told them I was dropping out of the race, Massey paid me a visit. He was furious."

"Why wouldn't you want to be the mayor?" I asked. "You stole the money years ago, and it's not like the others could have turned you in without implicating themselves."

Waterford hesitated and then said, "It wasn't simply the money. The higher the profile, the greater the scrutiny. Eventually, someone would have done more digging."

I suddenly realized what he meant. He'd implied most of the men had agreed to take the money. *Most.*

"Lance McKay," I said, recalling the name of the other man who had been with them in the hills.

Waterford nodded. "Now you get it. The company isn't Trident IV."

"What did you do?" I said, my eyes wide.

He didn't respond but looked at his watch.

"What was your plan?" I asked. "Use this case, this opportunity, to get these guys off your back? Were you expecting Trevor and me to bail you out somehow? You and your criminal counterparts couldn't settle things on your own, so you decided to call in the cavalry to save you?"

Waterford tried to laugh but couldn't manage the act.

"What's so funny?" I said.

"The cavalry," he replied. "As if you two are heroes." He put pressure on his wound and winced hard. "Do you really think you're the good guys?"

I didn't know what to say.

He continued, "You aren't the good guys. No. You two are simply better than the worst of us."

Waterford glanced at his watch again.

"What have you done?" I asked.

"It won't be long now. I know what he did in Pittsburgh when he lost someone he loved. I suspect he had something to do with that large explosion just over a year ago down here in Savannah. I wouldn't be surprised if that had something to do with him defending you. No, it won't be long now."

I asked again, my words slow and deliberate. "What did you do?"

Waterford locked eyes with me. In those eyes, I saw more tenacity than I'd seen at any other time.

"I did what I do best," he said. "I called in a strike."

Chapter 31

Trevor Galloway

"Oh, come on!" I exclaimed as I took another turn and checked the mirror. I'd been watching everyone in the marina and not one head had been turned in my direction. I knew damn well the local PDs weren't going to spend money putting GPS trackers on all of their cars, so someone had to have started tailing me as I left the scene. I supposed it wouldn't have been too difficult to track me if one had a police scanner since I'm sure my name had been mentioned. Anyone could discover my location. Then, someone could have parked near the exit of the marina and watched as I pulled away. In my state of mind, I wouldn't have necessarily noticed. Calendro was in custody, so who in the name of God was on my ass? I was already on Whitemarsh Island and didn't have time for this nonsense.

I sped up a little and saw a sign marking the entrance to a parking lot of a YMCA. The entranceway was heavily wooded on each side, so I made a quick turn off Johnny Mercer Boulevard into the parking lot. From what I could tell, the lot was empty, which was good since I didn't want any innocents getting hurt if whoever was following me decided to open fire.

Twenty yards into the entranceway, I slammed the brakes. The other car hadn't caught up to where the driver would be able to see me, so I left the car running, bailed out, and darted into the woods. I backtracked toward the entrance of the lot. From the bushes, I watched as the Chevy sedan turned the corner and then the driver hit the brakes, realizing my car was stopped up ahead. My tail crept along slowly as I pushed my way out of the shrubs and grabbed one of the green metal bars sticking out of the ground near the YMCA sign. I didn't know what in the world the things were called. In Pennsylvania, people used them to hold up snow fencing. In Savannah, I was going to use one to bash someone's head in. I love multiuse tools.

The Chevy continued to edge up, and I crept along the wood line on the passenger side, trying to stay in the driver's blind spot. The car came to a complete stop ten yards behind mine. This was the worst surveillance job ever. He had to know I would have spotted him by now. What was this person doing? I stayed crouched down and began moving toward the back of the car with the intent of smashing his window and then possibly his skull. I'd made it two steps when I heard the sound of a car door. I stood and watched as the drug gang enforcer who had been trying to plant the bomb on my car stepped out of the car.

From my angle, I could see he had a confused expression on his face. His head wasn't on a swivel and his situational awareness was terrible. I started moving fast, hoping the noise of both of our engines would cover my footfalls. He spun, gun in hand, as I made it to him. Using the metal bar, I slammed it down on his forearm and the gun clattered to the blacktop. I've discovered that when people have striking weapons like sticks or, let's say, metal bars, they tend to make the mistake of trying to hit their opponent with big sweeping strikes. The problem with those types of moves is that they require a lot of motion, which means the intent is telegraphed ahead of time. Also, they can be blocked or ducked. I wasn't going to make that mistake. I jabbed the steel bar into his nose. It broke instantly. The nose, I mean. The metal bar was fine.

The enforcer covered his face and dropped to his knees. I

started to kick him but opted to stop and pick up the gun.

"Do not kill me," he said in accented English.

"Why shouldn't I?"

"The case."

"That seems like a good reason," I said.

His hands were still on his face and he lowered them enough to look at me through confused, watery eyes that would be blackened circles in the morning.

"I am here to make offer."

I pointed the gun at his head but made sure I stayed out of arm's reach. "I know who you work for. You tell them that when I'm finished with my business here, I'm coming up north to end all of you. Do you hear me?"

"No war," he said. "New management."

Now I took a step back. "What?"

"We are here to make deal. No more war. Too many…how you say? Casualties. The man who brought your photo to us."

"Mr. Simon," I said, remembering the man who had put the EEDC onto my trail by letting them know I was in Savannah.

"He did not tell us his name. The man did not know how things changed after what you did in Pennsylvania. Word came down from the top. No more war with Tin Man. When photo was brought to us, then we knew the man would tell you and figured you would come hunt us down, thinking we would come after you. We waited for over a year, but you never attacked. Finally, management got tired of waiting and sent me, Sergei, to ask you to take deal."

I tried to digest what Sergei was saying. "You're not an enforcer?"

"No. I am courier." Sergei lowered his hands and checked them for blood. Now I saw he was no more than twenty years old. He said, almost bashfully, "But, I am trying to get into law school."

I couldn't believe it. Throughout the past year, Bethany and I had been on full alert, expecting an attack from a drug gang that had apparently been waiting up north—afraid of...*me*.

"What is in that silver case you've been carrying around?"

Sergei started to stand and stopped himself. "May I?" he asked. "I have no more weapons. I only carried the gun because I did not want you to kill me. When you were shooting at me before, I intentionally missed you. I only wanted to get away."

I nodded but kept the gun trained on him. He walked to the back door of the car, one hand pinching his nose. He opened the door, withdrew the case, and tried to hand it to me.

"I don't think so," I said. "You open it."

He set the case on the trunk of the car and took his right hand off his nose long enough to work the latches on both sides of the case. I stepped back as he lifted the lid and then strode forward when fire and brimstone didn't erupt.

Money. Lots and lots of money.

"Two million U.S. dollars. Management hopes that will be acceptable."

"Back up," I said.

The money certainly looked real. I reached out to touch it and then stopped myself.

"Run your hands over the bills and thumb through the stacks."

Sergei delayed, wondering what I was up to.

"Do it," I said.

I backed up and watched as he handled some of the bills.

"Okay, that's enough," I told him.

We stood there in silence for a minute or two. I'd needed to make sure the money hadn't been covered with something like fentanyl that could seep through my skin and kill me on the spot. Sergei didn't appear to be affected and he didn't seem concerned about handling the money.

Sergei looked around nervously until I said, "Then I'm done with you people? Forever?"

"Da," said Sergei. Then, in English, "Yes. Our business model is transitioning anyway. The organization's management is interested in investing in legitimate enterprises and removing itself from...other interests."

I closed the case and started to press the latches closed. I stopped and tapped my new gun on the case.

"Is something wrong?" asked Sergei. "Is the amount not acceptable?"

"You said *we*."

"I do not—"

"You said *we* are here to make a deal."

"Yes," said Sergei. "I travel here with three associates. They have been helping me watch you. Also, to be honest, they are here to replace me should you kill me."

"Did any of you sneak around my house a while back?"

Sergei appeared embarrassed. "I am afraid so. I came to your back door and thought about knocking but lost my nerve that day. I...you...well, you are somewhat of a cautionary tale to many of those in our organization. A boogie man, so to speak. My associates had good fun with me over my cowardice that day."

"These three men. Are they couriers as well?"

"No, no. They are more of the old school, if you get my meaning."

"Enforcers?" I asked.

"Not enforcers, but they are certainly hardened. I believe one is former Polish GROM. That is Special Forces. One did some mercenary work and the other is just a lunatic."

"No deal," I said.

Sergei's face fell. "I do not understand. Is there something wrong with the arrangement? I do not want to return having failed in my assignment."

"Then, let's negotiate," I said. "First off, I think this case is a little too heavy for me."

Chapter 32

Bethany Nolan

Mays burst back into the room and he wasn't alone. Filing in behind him were an irritated-looking Mark Altman and a red-faced Richard Massey. Mays closed the door behind the three while Massey took up a position directly in front of Waterford.

"You stupid bastard."

"Good to see you too, Rick," said Waterford without looking up.

"We could have had a good thing here, but now you've really gone and done it. A P.I.? You brought a P.I. in on this?"

"I don't know anything," I fibbed. "He shot me, which is a pretty strong indicator that I'm not on his side."

"Shut up," Massey commanded. "All you had to do was throw some business our way."

"And pay your dumb asses every once in a while because you don't have any business sense," Waterford shot back.

"This is stupid," I said, defying my order to shut up. "All of you are guilty of stealing that money."

They all turned to me.

"Okay. I might know a little *now*. He just told me. It seems to me you're equally as culpable in whatever happened over there, so I don't see how any of you can blackmail the other."

Now the younger one of the group, Mark Altman, stepped forward. "Because we didn't call in the strike that killed McKay. That's all on your friend, Sebastian."

Massey said, "Quiet, Mark." However, Altman kept talking.

"McKay wasn't taking any of the money, but he would have kept his mouth shut. He went into that building to do one last check while the three of us finished loading the money in our vehicle after that part of the town was clear. Sebastian knew he was in there and he timed the strike to kill McKay on purpose. We were going to say the blast took out weapons that had been left behind and then if word got around that money was missing, we'd simply say, 'Oops. It must have gone up in the blast.' At least this cold prick let us clear out the civilians before he turned the place to rubble."

Altman looked at me. "You see, we could always deny we took the money. Yeah, there was an investigation, but nothing ever stuck. But Waterford was always under a cloud for McKay's *accidental* death. If any one of us breathed a word that it was intentional and made up a reason for it—a personal feud, fight over a woman, whatever—people would be looking at him for murder."

"It was an accident," said Waterford, weakly.

"Bullshit," said Massey. "None of us bought it then and nobody is going to buy it now. I should have put a bullet in your head that day instead of your thigh."

Well, that might have explained Waterford's occasional limp, I thought.

Waterford said, "I thought he got out with you guys."

I looked at Waterford and tried to gage his sincerity. For the life of me, I couldn't tell if he was being truthful.

Massey kneeled in front of Waterford. "You see, Sebastian. You've put us in an impossible position here. It appears you aren't going to play ball with us and now you've brought a third party into the mix. All in all, it's a cluster."

Massey reached behind his back and produced a gun.

"The boys and I talked it over and…well, I guess there's not much more to say."

He pointed the gun at Waterford. I closed my eyes and anticipated the blast. Instead, I heard…a sound much more annoying. It was a car alarm. The sound it was making had to be akin to a donkey trying to sing an opera, and it seemed it was coming from near the exterior door."

Massey turned to Mays and Altman, jutting his chin toward the door. "Go check it out."

Both men went outside, pistols in hand. Massey remained in a kneeling position, eyeing us both.

Oh, Trevor, I thought. *Don't be on a suicide mission.*

A multitude of shots rang out, and I heard a voice I thought was Altman's. "We've got multiple contacts out here! Three or four. In the woods! They're spread out!"

Multiple contacts? Three or four? If Trevor had brought the cops with him, they would have announced themselves. He didn't have any friends other than Chase. I was sure none of Trevor's hallucinations had figured out how to manifest themselves into the real world—thank God. So…who was attacking Trident III? The room went dark for a second before an emergency light mounted high in the corner powered on.

Massey looked at Waterford. "Who's out there?"

Waterford managed a grin but didn't speak. The former SEAL then turned to me, pointed the gun at my face, and repeated the question.

"Probably the police," I said innocently.

"Cops don't come out shooting," he said. "Cops have rules of engagement. Who did you bring?"

With a dumfounded expression, I said, "I'm as lost as you are in all of this!"

Massey stood, retrieved a set of keys from a pocket, and walked over to the interior door that led to the Trident III office. He unlocked the door, stepped through, and I heard a lock shift back into place. I assumed he was heading out another door to help his associates who, from the sounds of things, were in a hell of a gunfight.

Five minutes passed by, during which Waterford and I heard one scream and a few low moans, but the gunfire persisted. I forced myself to my feet, unsure what to do, but aching to do *something*. The thought occurred to me to try the exterior door and possibly escape during the chaos of the gunfight. However, as soon as I took a step in that direction, three loud *clanks* on the door that had to have been bullets flattening against the metal informed me trying to run that direction was not a viable option.

Underneath the clattering of shots, I heard a rattling at the interior door and figured Massey was returning. Once again, I looked around the room in vain for a weapon to use. Being unable to find one, I moved beside the door and decided if I was going to go down, I would go down swinging. With the overhead lights out, it was a little darker, but there was no hiding other than to get behind the door and hope for the best. I'd lost a lot of blood and felt too weak to do much damage, but I'd try my best.

I heard the noise of the deadbolt moving as Massey unlocked it from his side, the side that didn't need a key. I saw the steel door handle tilt down. Finally, the hinges let out a light creak and the door edged open. With my left hand poised for action, I waited for either his gun to appear, so I could grab it, or his nose to present itself, so I could smash it with a palm strike. I hoped I had the strength for one good move before I would get overpowered or pass out.

The door moved six inches and then four more. Then…it stopped. Damn it. He had to be peering into the room. He would see that I wasn't on the floor, and any hopes I had for having gained the element of surprise were gone. My heart sank.

"Sweetheart, if you're in here and behind the door, please don't pummel me."

My heart leapt.

"I'm here," I said. "I'm right here."

Trevor came around the door and I saw he didn't look much better than I did.

"What happened to you?" I asked.

"The 9-1-1 killer hit me with a car. He's in jail now." Trevor's eyes fell to my right hand, which was covering my new injury. "What happened to you?"

"I got shot. Again."

"Trident III?"

I shook my head. Now, Trevor's eyes found Waterford who was watching us from his position on the floor. I saw the gun in Trevor's hand and could tell it wasn't one of mine.

Trevor stepped toward Waterford and raised the gun. "I don't know the whole story, but I'll fill in the blanks later."

I placed my hands on top of the weapon and our eyes met. We didn't speak, but this time we didn't need to say the words. Maybe this was a turning point for us. Life had thrown us together under the strangest of circumstances. We had made tough calls and our hands were nowhere close to clean.

Can you live with the things you have done? That's the question everyone always asks themselves, isn't it? The question is common, but nonsensical. Trevor and I could because we had to. Besides, by the time you have asked that question, you've done at least *some* living after whatever bad thing you've done, thus proving you can carry on. No. The better question is: *Can you live with who you are trying to be?* Having been bad is hard. Working to be better is harder, but maybe you end up paying a little less in baggage fees at the end of the day.

Without a word, Trevor lowered the gun. For once, he lowered the gun.

"He's in bad shape," I said.

Trevor pulled out his cell phone. "Now that I know what the deal is, I'll call in the police and get some ambulances started this way."

He spoke quickly and factually to the dispatcher but had to

repeat himself several times.

"Did you get that?" Trevor said into the phone before pulling it down from his face and staring at the screen.

"Are they coming?" I asked.

"I think so. My phone has been through a lot. It cut out when I was giving the address, but I think she heard me."

"We can't risk waiting here," I said. "We have to run."

The shots outside were dying down. I heard two in quick succession and then nothing.

"Trevor," I said.

"Yes."

"If the police aren't outside, then who has been out there battling it out with Trident III?"

"That's part of the drug gang that wanted to kill me before. I paid them a million dollars tonight to help us. We're cool now."

I stared at him, hating the fact he could always maintain a stoic expression.

"Fine," I said. "Don't tell me. We'll talk about it later."

Trevor's phone rang and he answered it.

"Sergei. Are you okay?" he said.

Sergei?

"How badly are you hurt? No. You've done enough. Get out of here. The cops are coming. Go. If the others are dead, then leave them. You've acted bravely and you should be proud. Okay, thanks for letting me know." Trevor paused, listened intently, and seemed concerned. "No. I said, no. Go to law school, kid." Trevor terminated the call and slid his phone back into his pocket.

"Mays is still alive," said Trevor. "He's wounded but outside that door." Trevor pointed toward the door leading outside. It looks like everyone else might be dead. You and I are getting out of here and hiding out until the police show up. I'm not getting into a close-quarters shootout with a former Navy SEAL if I can help it."

"What about him?" I said, nodding toward Waterford.

Trevor held out his hands, one holding the pistol. "Well, I didn't *shoot* him."

Better. I thought. *Not great. But better. Baby steps.*

Chapter 33

Trevor Galloway

"Any chance Mays is going to call it a day if he spots us?" I asked Bethany.

"I know too much," I said. "They helped cover up a possible homicide in Iraq and stole a lot of money while they were over there. If Mays gets a chance, he's going to kill me for sure."

"That won't happen," I whispered in the darkness.

One of Sergei's guys had insisted that cutting the power to the entire strip mall was a good idea. Since most of the old storefronts were glass walls, I couldn't exactly sneak through the building if it was lit up like Las Vegas. The plan had seemed logical and I wanted there to be as much confusion as possible once it appeared the Trident III crew was on scene along with Waterford. As we moved into the sporadic darkness of the main Trident III office space, I wasn't thrilled with the outcome of the plan. It didn't seem like most of the emergency lights were working and I couldn't see much of anything. I knew from my previous surveillance of the strip mall that we should be able to move from one area of the building to the other and get some distance from Mays.

Under normal circumstances, bringing a small hit squad and cutting the power could have seemed like overkill. But these were former Special Forces soldiers and the report Chase had obtained detailed an investigation into the accidental death of a SEAL team member that had been on a mission in Iraq with Waterford, Massey, Mays, and Altman. It didn't take a genius to figure out that if Waterford had been acting as if he didn't have any close ties to any of the Trident III men and was trying to get me into a deadly confrontation with them, then their relationship had soured in a big way. I knew Waterford was using Bethany as some sort of pawn, but I wasn't sure where Trident III stood.

With the absence of gunfire, the night had gotten deathly quiet. As we moved from the Trident III office space and into the next business area, the darkness was overwhelming. I slid into the room and Bethany held at the entryway. Only the few lights coming in from the glass storefront windows provided light. I stopped and listened carefully, knowing that my hearing was my best weapon. Mays had been firing a weapon and his hearing had to have been affected considerably. Sure it was dark as could be, but this was okay. As long as I could pick up the slightest noise, I had this one single advantage.

My body tensed and I ducked partially as the blast of sound seemed to echo everywhere. It was deafening, rhythmic, and familiar. I spun to Bethany, who for some reason, wasn't reacting at all other than to look at me with a curious expression. The music, yes, music was coming from the next section of the strip mall. I recognized the guitars, the drums, the distinct tones of Joe Elliot's vocals. The song was *Armageddon It* by Def Leppard, from their 1987 *Hysteria* album.

I kept my eyes on Bethany who was confused as to my reaction and mouthing, "What?"

Then I made myself look across the room to the open doorway that led to the next section of the building. My eyes struggled to adjust as the figure slowly rounded a corner of the doorframe. Even in the shadows I could see the long hair, the denim jacket, the hint of tattoos on the right side of his neck. I couldn't see the other side of his neck because hefted on his left shoulder he carried a gigantic boom box. He strode with the portable stereo in a manner I hadn't seen since the eighties. The electric guitars screeched and the bass boomed as he walked toward me with confidence. When he was within a few feet, I saw the smirk on his face and the blackness in his still-dead eyes. He reached up with his free hand and turned a knob on the boom box. The volume lowered to a more tolerable level.

"It has been too long, my friend."

I turned back to Bethany. "Let's keep moving."

"What's wrong?" she asked.

"Just keep going."

As soon as I put a foot forward, he twisted the knob and the volume increased. My head felt like it was imploding and exploding at the same time. I dropped to a knee and placed one hand on my head. The volume decreased again.

"Do not be rude," said the man. "I have helped you before. Maybe I'm here to help you again."

This was true. He had helped me before. However, I had a strong feeling that was not the case this time around.

"Trevor," I heard Bethany say, although it was difficult with the damn music playing. "What's happening?"

"He's here," I said.

She looked around. "Mays? Where?"

"No. Lukas. He's directly in front of me and is being difficult."

Bethany exhaled. "I know this seems like an obvious statement to make, but he's not really there. You can walk around him. Or through him." She pointed to her side. "I'm bleeding here, Trevor. I don't really care how we get past your dead enemy, Lukas Derela, but we're getting past him."

I stood and tried to take another step. Again, the music increased to a paralyzing level and I dropped back to a knee.

"He's stopping me," I said.

Bethany looked at me, her expression a mix of amazement, disbelief, anger, and frustration. "How could he possibly be stopping you?"

I opened my mouth and started to give her the details, then realized how it was going to sound.

"He's blasting a loud noise that's somehow keeping me from moving forward," I explained, trying to keep things simple and a little less ridiculous.

I raised my eyes to the drug dealer I'd killed so many years ago. "Let me go," I said.

Derela laughed. Half of his teeth were black and several were chipped. "Let you go from where?" he asked, his Lithuanian accent as heavy as I remembered.

I wasn't sure of the meaning of his question, since I thought my intent to get out of the building was obvious.

"I need to get out of here. If I die here, you no longer exist," I tried to reason.

The dealer clicked his tongue. "But where is here, Mr. Galloway? This room? This building?" He waved his right arm around. "Perhaps you wish to leave Savannah?"

"All of those sound good right now," I said.

"Because you ended up here after what you did in Pittsburgh."

"What's your point?" I asked.

Bethany, hearing only my side of the conversation, said, "Trevor, we really need to get going."

"Do you think you paid for what you did up there?" he asked.

"You know I did."

Once again, he clicked his tongue. "Three years. You took so many lives, yet you spent only three years in a hospital for crazy people. Does that seem right to you?"

"That's how it worked," I said.

Derela paused, then reached up and turned the volume down lower. "Is it?" he asked.

"I...yes," I said without conviction.

"Then you emerged back into the world to work a case involving a man running for president of the United States." Derela pointed to Bethany. "You meet a beautiful girl who is much too young for you. Both of you escape to another city and now my old colleagues forgive you and pay you a lot of money to leave them alone."

I nodded, or thought I nodded.

"You are a man of logic, Mr. Galloway. You appreciate facts and details. Well, as the expression goes, the devil is in these details."

"What are you saying?" I asked.

"You ask a lot of questions of a lot of people," said Derela. "But do you ever ask yourself the most important one?"

I swallowed hard and my stomach turned.

He'll get inside your head, I heard Lucile say from somewhere.

Derela said, "You say you want to leave this room, Mr. Galloway. But did you ever really leave that hospital room in Pittsburgh?"

I looked over at Bethany. Far too beautiful to be with someone like me. She looked back at me, almost pleadingly. Her eyes said, *move.*

"There is only one escape for you—for us—Trevor," said Derela, causing me to turn back to him. "If you turn that gun on yourself, perhaps you will wake up from the state you are in and maybe, just maybe, you will get out of the hospital someday."

Lucile's voice again. *He's coming to end it all.*

Derela wasn't wrong. I hadn't paid an appropriate price for my sins and many of the events I'd experienced over the past few years were hard to believe. Was it possible? Was I still locked up in some hospital room? Was a team of doctors monitoring me while I sat around in catatonic state? Was I a case study for young psychiatrists who needed to learn about homicidal maniacs and psychological breaks?

"None of this is real?" I said.

"Now you're getting it," hissed Derela.

"What?" exclaimed Bethany. "Hey, Trevor. I need you to

come back to Earth right now. We have a situation."

"So, all of the past five years…it's all been a lie."

"That's right," said the dealer.

Out of the corner of my eye, I saw a form move in the shadows behind Derela. I didn't focus on it. I didn't need to. Somehow, I knew what it was.

"That's why everything seemed to change after I killed all of those people. Probably because of all the drugs they are pumping into me since I'm still in the psych ward. Right?"

"That is correct," said Derela.

I nodded. "Then tell me something. How is it that I started seeing you long before I went into the psych ward and I'm still seeing you today? Are you some sort of bulletproof hallucination? Why did everything else in my mind change, but yet I'm still seeing your dead, ugly ass?"

Derela's grin faded for a moment before he regained his arrogance. "Oh, well. You cannot blame a guy for trying."

This was real. Bethany was real and that meant she was bleeding out and we had to get out of this place. I got to my feet and Derela's hand went back to the knob that controlled the volume. I raised my gun and he let out a laugh.

"We are at an impasse," he said. "You were right about one thing. I am bulletproof."

The form approaching from behind Derela moved closer and I locked eyes with him.

"Bethany is always telling me I don't have enough friends. But I have to say, I believe in quality over quantity."

In a flash of motion, Derela's head snapped back and the boom box fell to the floor, the music stopping. The drug dealer struggled against his much-smaller attacker, but she had the advantages of surprise, a lower center of gravity, and of having a piano wire tightening around his neck. Deep in my mind, I felt I was willing it to happen, yet I had the odd sense it was out of my control. Lucile—quiet, peaceful Lucile, with the voice of an angel, was choking the life out of my worst enemy and was not showing one iota of emotion while doing it. Thirty seconds later, Derela was dead on the floor, and Lucile was gesturing that Bethany and I should move to the next doorway.

"We can go now," I said to Bethany.

"Are you sure?"

"Yeah. Lukas is dead."

"Again? Wait. Who killed him?"

"Lucile."

"Luc—" Bethany began. "Sweet, signing Lucile?"

"She's got a heavy metal side," I said. "Come on."

We made it through three more office spaces and decided to chance a back exit out of the building. The police had to arrive soon and then, other than having a lot of explaining to do, we'd be all right. I led through what I'd hope would be our final doorway. It looked as if the area had once been used for retail clothing sales but was now filled with open cardboard boxes. It seemed Trident III was unloading and sorting some of their gear in this area. This room was even darker than the others but, having not heard any noises, I moved into the room, gun at the ready.

I'd like to explain what happened, but all I know was I had been holding the gun, then I wasn't, and then I'd been hit incredibly hard in the face. I heard Bethany get into the fray and she was tossed across a table, knocking over several cardboard boxes, spilling their contents. When I came up in a fighting stance, Richard Massey was very much still alive and coming toward me. I threw two quick jabs, which he dodged. He then countered with a right to the ribcage that I partially blocked. Massey moved in, attempting to get me into some sort of submission hold, but I attempted to kick him in the groin. He blocked the kick but backed up and reset in his approach.

I was a good fighter, but he was obviously better. Assuming Massey had a gun earlier, he must have lost it in the battle or run out of ammo. However, if Mays was still alive and out there somewhere, then I didn't have time to dance around with Massey.

"The cops are coming," I said. "You can still run."

"I can make up a story as long as there are no witnesses," he said.

Good point.

He feigned as if he was about to jab and then swept my leg from under me. Now I was in real trouble. Massey was on top of me before I could catch my breath and he had a hand squeezing my windpipe. I was doing what I could to get air, but he had both leverage and training. I opened my eyes one last time and saw a knife plunge into the side of Massey's head. His body slumped down onto me and I pushed it off as I gasped for air.

Bethany looked down at me. "One of those boxes over there had folding knives. Handy. Want one?"

"Sure."

We made it out the back door and looped around to the far side of the lot where Bethany had said Waterford had parked his car. Sirens sounded in the distance.

"We'll stay here out of sight until the police get here," I said. "It should only be another couple of minutes. How are you doing?"

"Not great, to tell you the truth," replied Bethany. "I need a vacation."

"You can afford it. We're millionaires."

"Seriously. What have you—"

A voice boomed behind us. "Did you kill Rick?"

It was John Mays. He was bleeding from a head wound and didn't seem happy about it. A Glock was dangling from his right hand. A trail of blood ran down his arm and droplets trickled off the end of the barrel. I had found my gun after the fight with Massey and it was in my hand. Mays eyed it and then my face.

"You've got to be kidding me," said Bethany. "I can't believe I'm going to say this, but I just want to go back to the hospital!"

"It's over," I said. "Everyone is dead. Waterford is probably dead by now. Keep your secrets. We just want to go home."

Mays stepped out into the parking lot and the sirens grew louder.

"What story could you possibly make up?" I asked. "There's too much carnage. Too much blood. How are you going to explain it to the police?"

Mays seemed to think about it, and I thought I had him. Then he raised the gun.

"Head wound," he said. "I don't remember a thing."

Before I could raise my gun and go out in a final blaze of glory, the sound of an engine came out of nowhere and a Chevy slammed into Mays, knocking him several yards away. I walked over and saw Mays's eyes were open and his body was not bending in natural ways. He was very much deceased.

The car door opened, and Sergei got out. "I know you told me I should leave, but Sergei did not want to abandon his post."

Like everyone else, Sergei was battered and bleeding from multiple locations. He limped, but it didn't seem any of his injuries were life-threatening.

"I thought I would at least wait and see if you make it out okay, just in case you need help. And look here. You needed my help!"

"Thank you, Sergei," I said.

He stuck out a hand to Bethany. "Hello. I am Sergei."

"Uh, Bethany."

"Oh, I know."

The sirens sounded as if they were nearly on top of us.

"You need to go," I said. I pointed toward a back access road I'd spotted previously. "Drive out that road. Don't speed. Just roll out of here like nothing happened."

"You got it, Mr. Galloway. Your briefcase will be at your house, like I told you." He took Bethany's hand again. "It was very nice to finally meet you in person."

With that, Sergei got into the car and drove away.

"And who the hell was that?" asked Bethany.

"Sergei," I said flatly. "I think he introduced himself."

"I hate you," she said.

"No, you don't."

"No, I don't."

We watched as the first patrol cars pulled in. The officers would clear the scene before the ambulances would move up next to the building. A trio of officers seemed to go around the corner to where the side door was, and I heard someone yell to another to get a rush on those ambulances. So, Waterford was still alive—at least for the time being.

Bethany said. "There are going to be a lot of questions."

"Yeah."

We walked to Waterford's car and sat on the hood. I put my arm around Bethany.

"Who was the 9-1-1 killer?" she asked.

"Remember the receptionist at the communications center? Her boyfriend. A firefighter."

"Huh." She pondered the information and then said, "Trevor."

"Yeah."

"Why do you smell like the river?"

I shrugged.

"Are we really rich?" she asked.

"I suppose."

"Oh," she replied.

Officers spotted us and started walking our way. They were cautious in their approach, their weapons drawn. We didn't move. We just watched them come.

"I was thinking we should get married," I said.

"Definitely," she said, looking ahead.

A few seconds passed by. "Is the drug gang really off our backs?"

"Looks that way."

"Money, freedom, marriage. All of that?"

"Yep."

"Wow," she said.

I squeezed her as tight as I dared, not wanting to hurt her.

"Then I guess we're good," she said.

I nodded and said, "We're...better."

ACKNOWLEDGMENTS

Thanks to Eric Campbell and Lance Wright at Down and Out Books for their continued support of this series. They have been a pleasure to work with for all of these years. I'm indebted to Freddie Clifton who lent me his insights into the nuances of how various police departments in the Savannah area communicate through the Chatham County 911 Center. Freddie also helped me with various other aspects of the book, but—as I've done with my other stories—I took various liberties with the layouts of buildings, security procedures, etc. as to help in the telling of the story and to not help any bad guys figure out how to do any harm. Michael Gerchak was kind enough to give this story an advance read and caught several mistakes. Thanks to him for his assistance.

Thanks to my colleagues at The Thrill Begins, to the International Thriller Writers, and to the Low Country chapter of Sisters in Crime. Writers are fantastic. It's a genuine pleasure to be in a field where ninety-nine percent of the people are jealous of someone else, but everyone seems to support one another. As always, I'm grateful to my wife, Kasia, for giving me the initial feedback on the manuscript. She's the one who has to muddle through my hastily typed double words, plotlines that hit dead-ends, and those times I get my own characters mixed up with one another.

Finally, thanks to all of you who have followed Trevor

Galloway through four novels. When I decided to develop his story into a series, I made the conscious choice to let him change as a character, rather than to remain static. You've seen his life, and his personality, change quite a bit since he arrived in *Bolt Action Remedy*. By allowing him to evolve, I took a risk, albeit a somewhat calculated one. I wagered that my readers would appreciate seeing his life change from book to book, since many of us enjoy fiction that in some way mirrors reality. You've stuck by Trevor, so I thank you and he does as well. But you're not getting a smile from either of us.

J.J. Hensley is a former police officer and former Special Agent with the U.S. Secret Service. He is the author of the novels *Resolve*, *Measure Twice*, *Chalk's Outline*, *Bolt Action Remedy*, and *Record Scratch*. He is also one of the contributors to the critically acclaimed novel in stories, *The Night of the Flood*.

Mr. Hensley's first novel *Resolve* was named one of the Best Books of 2013 by Suspense Magazine and was named a Thriller Award finalist for Best First Novel.

He is a member of the International Thriller Writers.

On the following pages are a few
more great titles from the
Down & Out Books publishing family.

For a complete list of books and to
sign up for our newsletter,
go to DownAndOutBooks.com.

Headstone's Folly
A John Headston Mystery
Robert J. Randisi

Down & Out Books
October 2020
978-1-64396-148-4

John Headston took a bad step 12 years ago, and it cost him his freedom and his career. But now that he's been pardoned, and has reopened his Headstone Detective Agency, he's ready to start again.

But into his office walks the woman who was the reason he lost it all, and she wants to use him again. She wants him to find out who's trying to kill her wealthy, older husband.

Will Headston risk it all again, or will he realize the folly of that action and turn her down?

Suicide Blonde
Three Novellas
Brian Thornton

Down & Out Books
October 2020
978-1-64396-044-9

Three Stories. Three Eras. Three Crimes.

A 1960s mob fixer is drawn into a Vegas fix that might just put the fix on him.

Dead Chinese immigrants wash up on the beaches of 1889 Seattle and one government official refuses to look the other way.

An Italian ex-galley slave, sometime thief, and full-time rogue masterminds a one-of-its kind jail break in 1581 Constantinople.

this gun from Norman Court
The Trevor English Series
Pablo D'Stair

All Due Respect, an imprint of
Down & Out Books
October 2020
978-1-64396-119-4

Reduced to life in skid-row shelters, petty thief Trevor English is apprehended by store-detective-cum-freelance-investigator Leonard Bellow. Turning a blind eye to his theft, Bellow offers Trevor a job doing reconnaissance work – an opportunity Trevor jumps at.

But in the world he has cornered himself in nothing is what it seems on the surface … except, he will realize, for Trevor English: deadbeat, easy mark, lamb to the slaughter.

White Trash and Dirty Dingoes
Jason Parent

Shotgun Honey, an imprint of
Down & Out Books
July 2020
978-1-64396-101-9

Gordon thought he'd found the girl of his dreams. But women like Sarah are tough to hang on to.

When she causes the disappearance of a mob boss's priceless Chihuahua, she disappears herself, and the odds Gordon will see his lover again shrivel like nuts in a polar plunge.

With both money and love lost, he's going to have to kill some SOBs to get them back.

www.ingramcontent.com/pod-product-compliance
Lightning Source LLC
Chambersburg PA
CBHW020251030426
42336CB00010B/712